out**dated**

Find Love That Lasts
When Dating Has Changed

JONATHAN "JP" POKLUDA

with Kevin McConaghy

BakerBooks

a division of Baker Publishing Group
Grand Rapids, Michigan

© 2021 by Jonathan Pokluda

Published by Baker Books
a division of Baker Publishing Group
PO Box 6287, Grand Rapids, MI 49516-6287
www.bakerbooks.com

Printed in the United States of America

Library of Congress Cataloging-in-Publication Data
Names: Pokluda, Jonathan, 1980– author.
Title: Outdated : find love that lasts when dating has changed / Jonathan "JP" Pokluda with Kevin McConaghy.
Description: Grand Rapids, Michigan : Baker Books, a division of Baker Publishing Group, 2021. | Includes bibliographical references.
Identifiers: LCCN 2020035437 | ISBN 9780801094958 (paperback) | ISBN 9781540901507 (casebound)
Subjects: LCSH: Single people—Conduct of life. | Dating (Social customs)—Religious aspects—Christianity.
Classification: LCC BV4596.S5 P65 2021 | DDC 646.7/708827—dc23
LC record available at https://lccn.loc.gov/2020035437

The author is represented by the literary agency of The Gates Group Literary Agency.

22 23 24 25 26 27   7

"Every Christian I know who isn't married yet is looking for dating advice. How to do this well in our day, with our technology and our culture, is a leading conversation, and honestly, JP is the leading expert. In this book, with kindness, compassion, and thoughtfulness, JP gives godly wisdom that walk us toward the relationships with God, others, and ourselves that we really want."

Annie F. Downs, bestselling author of *100 Days to Brave* and host of *That Sounds Fun* podcast

"Modern dating is already outdated. It causes pain and problems and leads to confusion and frustration. In *Outdated*, JP reveals that the Bible is full of wisdom principles you can use to find incredible joy in dating—and a lasting love for life. Some people think that following what is fashionable in dating is the way to go. The truth is *Outdated* has the timeless secrets of relationship favor for you."

Kyle Idleman, author *Not a Fan* and *Don't Give Up*

"Everything about dating has changed, and there is no one I trust more to help you navigate it than JP! He is a leader for the next generation."

Jennie Allen, *New York Times* bestselling author of *Get Out of Your Head* and founder and visionary of IF:Gathering

"If you are dating, you need this book in your life! Throughout this book, JP is constantly pointing you to the truth that's worth standing on while helping you dismantle the lies culture has sold us about dating. You can date and glorify God while doing it! Let this book be a guide to you on that journey!"

Jamie Ivey, bestselling author and podcaster

"*Confusion* and *disappointment* are the two main words I hear from young adults when chatting about dating and relationships in today's landscape. Yet there also isn't much wisdom or good voices out there. That's why I love *Outdated* and JP. This book is powerful, tactical, wise, and inspiring all at the same time. We are due for a fresh vision on all things dating and relationship related, and JP delivers that to us in this amazing book."

Jefferson Bethke, author of *Take Back Your Family*

"One thing is for certain: dating in today's culture is confusing, twisted, and often filled with frustration and disappointment. Something needs to change. *Outdated* offers a clear and practical roadmap for dating in a new way. Unafraid of being incredibly forward, JP is powerfully direct in his words as he dismantles some of the top dating myths in culture today and replaces them with powerful, life-altering truth. If you are single or dating, without question you need this book in your hands."

Kait Warman, author of *Thank You for Rejecting Me*, relationship coach, and founder of Heart of Dating

"If only I could go back and give this book to my college self! JP's practical wisdom and insight would have saved me from so much unnecessary pain. Here is a textbook on dating that is saturated with Scripture, pregnant with hope, and authenticated by real life experience. I commend *Outdated* to any and every young adult. I beg you to view it as required reading for the sake of your joy. There is no need to risk several wrong turns when JP is handing you a map. Keep this resource close by throughout young adulthood."

Timothy Ateek, executive director of Breakaway Ministries

"Next to the decision to follow Jesus, there is no decision more significant that who you will marry. This book is a must-read for anyone trying to successfully navigate love, sex, dating, and marriage."

David Marvin, leader of The Porch

"*Outdated* is a valuable resource to those who are navigating the tumultuous waters of dating and relationships in today's world! My friend JP gives voice to the struggles that many people face in dating and offers helpful, specific direction on what it looks like to change the landscape of dating and relationships for the better."

Ben Stuart, pastor of Passion City Church DC and author of *Single, Dating, Engaged, Married*

To someone who has been ghosted and feels forgotten.
To anyone looking for a road map to dating in the church.
For the helpless romantic who hasn't lost hope.
This was written for you.

Jonathan Pokluda

Contents

Contents

Introduction

Everyone wants to be loved.

I can't think of a truer statement of human nature than that. It is perhaps our greatest desire. Although I already knew this to be true, it came into full view for me as I watched thousands of twenty- and thirtysomethings crowd into a room every Tuesday for worship and teaching from the Bible at a gathering called The Porch. The reason so many people would attend The Porch in addition to their regular Sunday services was that these Tuesday evenings were focused on the topics and issues most relevant to people in their twenties and thirties. The sermons would cover things like career decisions, managing finances, finding your purpose, making an impact with your life, overcoming addictions—no subject was off-limits, and over the years we covered just about every topic you could think of, in addition to teaching through books of the Bible.

However, there was one topic that always stood out.

About once a year, we'd have a series about dating. And without fail, those were always the most-anticipated, most-attended, most-talked-about sermons of the year. The auditorium would be full to the rafters. We streamed all of our services online and posted them as podcasts, and the dating talks would always get the highest viewership and the most downloads. So many people would come forward after the service looking for advice, or email or call us with questions during the following days, that we had to extend each dating series by a week so that we could have one Tuesday devoted just to answering people's questions in a rapid-fire format. And after seeing this happen over and over again for a decade at The Porch, a year ago I moved to a college town to lead another church that also has a weekly young adult ministry—and the same thing is happening here. I even started doing a weekly Q&A on Instagram, and though people can ask literally anything, I end up getting hundreds of questions each week about relationships and dating.

In other words, no other issue facing single people today—nothing else in all of the human experience—causes as much interest, angst, confusion, curiosity, questioning, and pain as dating. It's the area single people want the most help in.

One reason people are so interested in dating is because they know it's important. Finding love is a top priority in life. And although most of us have parents and other family members who already love us, somehow that isn't enough. We want a different kind of love. We want someone to *choose* to love us, not love us because they are related to us. In fact, we want someone to choose to be related to us, through marriage. We want the lifetime, unconditional level of love we would get from family but also want it to be based entirely on who we are rather than to whom we were born.

Many of us want that kind of love—love that lasts—more than anything. But it seems like it's become the most difficult thing in the world to find. That's the other reason why people are so interested in dating advice: we, as a society, are getting increasingly bad at it. The change is kind of dramatic. In 1960, 65 percent of all people ages eighteen to thirty-two were married; in 2013, only 26 percent were.[1] And although some people try to explain this away by claiming that today's young adults simply don't want to get married, the same study says that, of the 74 percent who aren't married, roughly seven in ten would like to be. People do want to get married; they're trying to reach that goal but are just not succeeding at it very often. Another study from Stanford found that different generations all have the same ideal age at which they'd like to get married; young adults today would prefer to marry at the same age as their grandparents' generation did.[2] Yet the average age at which people first get married has increased from 21.5 years old in 1960 to 28.9 years old in 2019,[3] meaning that it now takes seven extra years of dating to find a marriage match. And once we are married, that doesn't necessarily mean we're married well: somewhere between a third and a half of all marriages end in divorce,[4] and obviously not all undivorced marriages are successful.

What's crazy about that is it seems like today's young adults should be really, really good at dating. Compared to previous generations, we have so many more choices and so much more information available to us. We have dating apps and websites designed to sort through the millions of available singles and supposedly help us find the algorithmically perfect match. We have an endless string of movies and

TV series showing us examples of how to date, including some where people literally compete to be the one to marry an eligible bachelor or bachelorette. And yet, by just about every measurable standard, we're continually getting worse at dating.

The problem is we're following the wrong examples. Almost from birth, we're told that dating and marriage are supposed to look a certain way. Our views on love and relationships are based just as much on fantasy—literally fairy tales—as they are on anything resembling real life. We watch actors playing fictional people fall in fictional love in fictional stories, and we think that somehow real life should be as dramatic as the movies.

When we move from fiction to reality, we don't fare much better, because the reality is that modern dating is a failure. It's not producing the results we want. If you obey all of the popular "rules" for dating and follow the supposedly good advice from the countless articles and videos and influencers on the subject—in other words, if you do the same things everyone else is doing—then you'll get the same outcomes as everyone else. And those outcomes, statistically, aren't that great.

Basically, we're believing in myths. We talk about things like "love at first sight," and finding "the one," and "happily ever after." We try to conform to modern society's standards and expectations for dating, even though modern society is terrible at forming relationships that last. By and large, we're doing dating wrong, and the results speak for themselves.

I've had a front-row seat to it all, first through my own dating mistakes (and trust me, I made *a lot* of them), and then through the tens of thousands of singles I've gotten to observe and minister to. I've seen what works and what (unfortunately) doesn't. Most importantly, I've learned about God's wisdom for life and relationships through studying the Bible, and have strived to share that with others so they can find success and avoid heartache in dating.

I remember giving one dating talk at The Porch years ago, when I was still relatively new on the job. Afterward, one young woman wanted to meet with me to discuss the message. I grabbed a friend and we sat down to hear what she had to say. She proceeded to go through my sermon point-by-point and explain how I was wrong about everything. You see, she figured she was pretty much an expert on dating, since she did it a lot and in her eyes had been successful at getting whichever guy she wanted. She'd even been married once, although that relationship had ended in divorce. There were also some other bumps in her dating road, such as a string of bad breakups, and the time she got pregnant and decided to get an abortion. So, after we finished listening to her tell me how I had it all wrong about dating, and how her way was better, I simply asked, "And how is that working out for you?"

(Spoiler alert: when she finally decided that her worldly way of dating wasn't working, and chose to try the godly way instead, she ended up marrying another good friend of mine in a ceremony that I had the honor to officiate. Not only that, but God has written an amazing story of redemption on her life.)

If you think you're happy with the results you're getting, there's no need to change. But most people *aren't* happy with the results they're getting in dating, and statistically it's not working for us on a society-wide level. You can't do the same things you've been doing, and the same things millions of other people have been doing, and expect to get different results. Don't think that *this* time will be different, or that somehow it will work for you when it hasn't worked for anyone else. If you want a different outcome, you need to provide a different input. You have to be willing to change.

A Different Way

The world may have a lot of rules for dating. But the Bible, which many people (wrongly) think of as a big book full of rules, has very few dating rules.

Partly, that's because dating as we know it didn't exist in Bible times. In fact, dating hasn't existed throughout most of history; the concept was only invented a little over a century ago. In the early 1900s, when it first came into fashion, the term *dating* was originally seen as a euphemism for prostitution, largely due to confusion because the two practices seemed so similar.[5] It is a new idea; most people throughout most of history managed to live, love, and marry successfully without ever "dating" anyone.

But just because modern dating wasn't really around when the Bible was written doesn't mean the Bible doesn't have anything relevant to say about the subject. It may not have many rules about dating, but the few it does have are very clearly applicable to our lives today. Plus, it is worth noting that those few rules highlight the most glaring ways in which modern dating tends to get things wrong, and that ignoring those rules is what causes the biggest problems and the most pain in dating. That's because any commands God gives us are for our own benefit. They are not at all meant to stifle our fun. Instead, they exist to point us toward life and help us avoid doing things that cause us emotional, physical, or relational harm.

Beside listing those relatively few clear sins to avoid, the Bible is full of wisdom principles we can use to find incredible life in dating. They are not so much rules to be followed as they are really good ideas that will never steer us wrong. Really, most of these would be considered common sense, but unfortunately sense is not all that common anymore, especially when it comes to something as emotionally charged as dating.

Essentially, we are given a lot of freedom in how we pursue relationships, but things go better for us when we follow God's advice.[a] As 1 Corinthians 10:23 says:

> "I have the right to do anything," you say—but not everything is beneficial. "I have the right to do anything"—but not everything is constructive.

You can ignore or try to rationalize away what the Bible says and do things your own way instead. But it will not go well for you.

It may seem ironic to say that something as old as the Bible holds the cure for what ails dating in the twenty-first century.

a. Although this book is written from a Christian perspective, I know that some readers will not be followers of Christ. If that includes you, welcome! I'm so glad you are here. Believe it or not, because God did create everything, and all things function according to his design, many of the suggestions in this book will still "work" even if you don't believe in him. That is why I often cite statistics; secular evidence verifies that God's plan for relationships is best. However, I don't want you to *only* have better dating relationships and a better marriage. No matter what happens—good or bad—in eighty or ninety years of life on earth, it's going to be just a blip compared to eternity. So make sure you get the eternity question right. With that in mind, you have my permission to jump to the end of the book and read the last chapter first, before coming back and reading the rest from here.

However, it is actually modern dating ideas that should be (and hopefully, for you, soon will be) considered outdated. Most of them are not really modern ideas, anyway; they are just repackages of the same lies people have always been tempted to fall for. Regardless, we've been doing dating this way for long enough to know the results. The experiment has been run, with millions and millions of repetitions each year, and the data shows it's not working. The principles in God's Word, on the other hand, have proven to be reliable. The Bible never becomes out of date, because it is the truth, and the truth doesn't change over time.

Trade the lies for truth. Start dating a different way.

What You'll Find

My entire purpose in writing this book is to help you date well and end up in a fantastic marriage, without all the pain and problems that dating so often causes. I'm not promising a fairy-tale ending, because that's fantasy, and we're all imperfect people living in a fallen world. But I think I can help you on the adventure of finding a God-honoring relationship, and it is a beautiful thing when two godly people commit to loving each other. It is something that I believe, for most people, is worth pursuing.

Throughout the book we'll look at the various myths, misconceptions, or mistakes that society promotes when it comes to relationships. Each chapter is named after a different outdated concept—the twelve most common lies people believe about dating—and then covers what wisdom would have us do instead. The goal is not to replace one man-made set of rules with another but rather to point toward the One who invented marriage, who created us to crave relationships, and who is the very embodiment of true love.

This book will give you practical advice you can apply today, in addition to a big-picture understanding of God's purposes for singleness, dating, and marriage. It will cover why you should date, whom you should date, and how you should date.

As you read, I would encourage you to share what you are learning. Invite those close to you to join you on the journey. I always recommend reading books like this in community with others who can spur you on and keep you accountable. Dialogue about it with them. Talk about what you agree with and what you disagree with. Share what is helpful with others. You could even post a picture on social media and let everyone know you are beginning a journey. They can watch your success, and you can invite those close to you to join you on it.

Grab some friends, grab some coffee, and let's get started.

PART 1

why we date

1

Dating for Fun

THE LIE: the purpose of dating is to have fun.

THE TRUTH: it's a lot more fun when you date with the right purpose.

I like to go shopping. I know that probably goes against all sorts of stereotypes, but I do. So, when a friend texted me one weekend and asked if I wanted to go to the outlet mall with him, my reply was, "Of course!"

He picked me up, and it wasn't until we were on our way that I asked him *why* we were going shopping. He said he was looking for a new rain jacket. It had been raining a lot over the previous weeks, and his old rain jacket had a hole in it, so he needed to get a new one. He figured the North Face outlet store was a good place to start looking. "Great," I said. "Outlet mall, here we come!"

Once we got there, it was clear that my friend was on a mission. As soon as he walked through the door, his eyes were scanning the store to identify where the jackets were located.

Once he spied the right section, he headed straight toward it, ignoring everything else he passed on his way there. And when he got to the jackets, he was solely concerned with finding one that would work for him. *Is it waterproof? Is it the right size? Is it a good enough quality? Does it have a hood?* If the answer to any of these was no, then there was no need for him to waste time even considering it. He was even looking for some kind of specific hood with a cinch strap, so that really narrowed down his search. He couldn't find what he needed at the first store, so he immediately left it and started looking for another option. "OK, there's a Columbia outlet. Let's go try that store."

He was looking for something very specific, but I wasn't really looking for anything at all—which really means I was looking at everything. While he knew exactly where to go and what to look for, I just kind of wandered around, seeing if anything caught my eye. I left him behind and went into other stores. *Oh man, check out this skateboard. Or this vest. Or over here, they have snowshoes! Do I need snowshoes? It hasn't really snowed here in, like, a decade. But maybe snowshoes would be cool to have.*

Both my friend and I were technically doing the same thing—"shopping"—but our experiences could hardly have been more different. He was on a mission; he had an objective and a purpose. I, on the other hand, was just playing around. I was shopping for fun. It was a form of entertainment for me. I had time to kill, I had endless options in front of me, and I thought maybe I could find something I could use that would bring me joy. And at the end of the day, my friend went home with exactly what he needed, a new rain jacket, and I went home with my seventeenth pair of sunglasses and a toy helicopter that broke the very next morning.

Dating for Fun

The biggest problem with dating is that far too many people approach it the same way I approached shopping that day. We just wander around, looking at anything and everything, not knowing what or who we might end up taking home with us (or who we might go home with). We're searching, but we're not searching for anything in particular. We're just out there, at the store or the bar or wherever, looking for something pretty that might catch our eye, or someone pretty we might catch the eye of. Little thought is given as to quality, or whether they are a good fit, or whether they're not just a slightly newer version of the same thing that's already failed us a dozen times before.

We're just dating for fun. We're looking for something—or, more accurately, someone—we can use to bring us pleasure. We may be looking for sex, attention, or a stroke to our ego, making us feel good that we can afford such a shiny object. But make no mistake: these people are just objects to us. When we date like this, we treat other people as things we can use for our own benefit. It goes both ways; the other person may be using us at the same time. But the fact that it's mutual doesn't make it any better for either party or any less likely to fail. If your goal is fun, fun is all you will get—until it's not fun anymore. That new, shiny object is no longer new to you, and it begins to lose its luster. As with any toy, the initial excitement wears off, and it becomes less fun to play with over time. So people throw it away, or exchange it for another new plaything—a process you can repeat over and over again, without ever getting anywhere. It may be temporarily fun, but I'm not sure we realize how costly that fun is.

The idea that the primary purpose of dating is to have fun is one of the myths our culture tells us. Dating is seen as a type of recreation, or just some kind of grown-up game we play. People may not always realize they treat dating this way, and indeed you may be thinking right now that you don't. But there's a really simple test for this: if your purpose in dating is anything other than marriage, then that is what you're doing. If you are dating in order to find someone to marry, then your goal is actually to *stop* dating around, because marriage would put an end to that. Once you are married, you will (hopefully) never go on a first date again. But if you're dating because on some level you enjoy the process, and marriage is just this incidental thing that might happen if things really work out perfectly, then your real goal in dating is to have fun. And so you continue to play the same games, chase the same experiences, and end up in the same places you've been. Until one day when you look up and think, *Wow. I've been doing this for a long time, and it hasn't gotten me anywhere.*

Evidence for the prevalence of this "dating for fun" mindset is everywhere. Why else would we expect it or accept it when people start dating in high school, junior high, or even earlier? Are you going to get married at age fourteen? No? Then where is this relationship really going to go over the next few months or years?[a]

And why else would you have people who, as adults, have been dating for five years (or more) without ever putting a ring on it? What, you can't figure out within a half decade

a. I'm not saying you can't possibly meet your future spouse as a child. But I am saying it is rare—certainly rarer than it used to be, when more people lived in small towns and tended to marry at a relatively younger age—and that, even in those cases, there is no need to "date" someone as a child. You can meet someone and get to know them as friends, but then wait until you are actually ready for marriage before dating them.

whether this person is worth marrying or not? If your goal from the start was marriage, then I'm afraid you're failing at that goal.[b] But if your goal was to have fun, and you're having fun not being married, then it suddenly makes sense. The idea also works its way into our vocabulary. People use slang like "he got game" in reference not just to sports but to dating. It means that someone has the ability to get someone of the opposite sex to say yes, not to marriage but to a short-term dating relationship and everything that goes with it. Because, face it, if someone dated one person successfully, where it actually led to a lifelong commitment in marriage, no one would ever say that person "had game." That's almost the opposite of having game. You "have game" only if you're treating dating as a game. Or you're a "player" only if you're playing a game—playing with other people, as if they were toys. It's childish. It's what happens when people become adults but never really mature and grow up. I see it all the time: you have thirty-year-old boys and girls out there playing with each other's hearts, usually in an effort to get to some other body part. Don't play like that. Don't be a child. Don't toy with others, and don't let yourself be toyed with. As Romans 12:9 says, "Love must be sincere."

Dating Is Not Fun

The tragic aspect of this "dating for fun" mentality is that dating around isn't all that fun.

I'm married now, but obviously I haven't always been married. I've lived through all the different relationship statuses: single, dating, and married (also single-while-sleeping-around

---

b. I'm sorry if that applies to you, but logically, it's true. And sometimes the truth hurts.

and dating-for-fun). I've also counseled a lot of other young adults through the issues associated with each stage. I've seen people do all of this wrong and invite incredible pain into their lives, and I've seen people do this really well and experience a life-giving marriage. So I can say from experience, and from observing the experiences of others: dating is awful. I mean, of the three options of singleness, dating, and marriage, dating is by far the least fun. By far. If you are having a blast dating around, you're probably doing it wrong.

Some of you single people may immediately object that singleness isn't much fun either, but that's just because you're so focused on wanting to *not* be single. Done right, singleness can be amazing. (More on that later.) Marriage, also, has been an awesome gift in my life. It takes work, but it's far better than the days when I was just dating.

Dating is like when you're looking for a job and are in the interview phase. It's not a fun phase. Who likes job interviews? You put on your uncomfortable interview clothes, perhaps your so-called power tie or pantsuit, and you walk into this awkward situation where it feels like the other attendees are judging you (because they are). You present yourself for their approval. You feel exposed and vulnerable. And then you go home, put on comfy pants, and stress about the results. *Are they going to call me back? I don't know. They said they would, but I don't know. Where's it going? Is it going anywhere? Maybe I should interview with some other people instead, even though that requires me to go through the same awkward process again, and again, and again.* You're just perpetually sitting in this vulnerable spot. That's dating. It's not fun.

What's fun is when you actually get the job. It's like, *OK, now I know I'm accepted. Now we're committed to each other. Now we've got something good.* But that's not dating anymore. That's marriage. I'm thankful every day that I am married and no longer have to go through the stress and mess that was my dating life.

Or, to use another shopping metaphor I once heard from my friend Jeff Bethke: if marriage is buying and dating is shopping, dating without the intention of marriage is shopping with no money. What's going to happen when you shop with no money? Either you're going home empty-handed or you're going to take something that isn't yours. Those are the only two possible outcomes.

Dating for Marriage

Instead of selfish and self-defeating "fun," the sole goal of dating should be marriage.

God invented marriage.[c] It's a gift from him,[d] and (for most people) it is worth pursuing. Singleness, also, can be a gift from God.[e] But dating was not created by God. Dating

c. In the creation account in Genesis 2:18, "The LORD God said, 'It is not good for the man to be alone. I will make a helper suitable for him.'" And Jesus said in Matthew 19:4–6 (while quoting from Gen. 1:27 and 2:24), "'Haven't you read,' he replied, 'that at the beginning the Creator "made them male and female," and said, "For this reason a man will leave his father and mother and be united to his wife, and the two will become one flesh"? So they are no longer two, but one flesh. Therefore what God has joined together, let no one separate.'"

d. Proverbs 18:22: "He who finds a wife finds what is good and receives favor from the LORD."

e. 1 Corinthians 7:7–9: "I wish that all of you were as I am. But each of you has your own gift from God; one has this gift, another has that. Now to the unmarried and the widows I say: it is good for them to stay unmarried, as I do. But if they cannot control themselves, they should marry, for it is better to marry than to burn with passion."

was invented by people, and is a relatively recent invention at that. It's a new category. It's not even in the Bible. Dating can be redeemed; it can fulfill a godly purpose. But only if we date with a purpose.

The only reason we should date is to get married. We date because God gave us the gift of marriage, and we're trying to get there.

That simple statement has some serious implications. If you don't want to be married, don't date. If you're not ready to be married right now (or in the very near future), then don't date right now.

All dating relationships will end in either marriage or a breakup. So if marriage is not a possibility, then breaking up will be a certainty. The only question is how long it will take before you break up. And in this case, a longer, seemingly more successful relationship is actually worse. It means that the eventual breakup (which, again, is *guaranteed* to happen) will just be more painful, with more emotional entanglements. And if the other person in the relationship actually *is* ready for marriage, as is often the case, then you've wasted months or even years of their life by leading them on. So, although I want to emphasize that you simply should not be dating if you are not ready for marriage, you should *at the very least* be honest with the other person from the start. In other words, you should tell them up front, "I'm going to break up with you whenever I feel like it." Indeed, that should be your pickup line. Because that's what you are asking them to sign up for. You're not going to marry them; you're going to break up with them. You want to use them for entertainment, because of how dating them makes you feel, and then leave them at some indeterminate point in the future. So just be honest about that. It will keep you from being a manipulator, a liar, and a user.

I've heard some people argue that dating someone when you know you're not going to marry them is somehow helpful, in that it allows people to learn what they like or don't like in a dating partner (and therefore, presumably, a spouse). I would say that's a very selfish way to use another person. Again, you'd have to be brutally honest about what you're doing and how you are using them from the very start, or else you are just intentionally toying with people and likely hurting them. I would also say there's a better way to determine what you should be looking for in a spouse, and I'll talk about that in later chapters.

Dating the Right People

Another principle related to "do not date unless marriage is a possibility for you" is that, if you are dating someone and realize the relationship will definitely not end in marriage, you should break up with that person. As in *immediately*. Otherwise you're just wasting time (both yours and theirs) and unnecessarily leading them on. It might seem harsh, but it's actually the kindest thing you could do for them. It minimizes the potential pain caused by a longer relationship. (There will be more on how to go about ending a dating relationship in chapter 10.)

This also means you should only start dating a person if they are someone you might possibly end up marrying. Now, I want to be clear here: I don't mean you have to know you're going to marry them before you begin dating them. (If you already knew that, you wouldn't need to date each other; you could just go ahead and get married.) I just mean that there has to be a possibility you could end up marrying them. That, based on what you know about them so far, they appear to make a good potential spouse. And then, as you get to know them better through dating, either you will confirm they are someone you want to marry (and you'll marry them), or you'll determine they're not someone you want to marry (and you'll break up).

When you're dating for marriage rather than dating for fun, you'll evaluate potential dating partners differently. You'll look for traits that would make them a good spouse, and you'll likely find this will narrow down your options considerably, which is a good thing.

When I went shopping with my friend that day at the outlet mall, I looked at everything. Every item, in every store, was a possibility. I could go home with anything. But very few of those things would be any good for me. They'd be a waste of time, money, and space, and I'd end up having to eventually get rid of them. My friend, on the other hand, had very specific parameters for what he was looking for. He knew what he needed, and he knew where to look for it. And with fewer options, it was easier for him to make a decision. He ended up happy with his purchase and satisfied with his overall shopping experience, because he found what he needed and didn't waste time in the process. It was, in other words, kind of fun for him.

Check Your Baggage

After our wedding ceremony, my wife and I went on a honeymoon to an all-inclusive resort in Playa del Carmen, Mexico.

We had never been to Mexico before and were not fully clear on what "all-inclusive" meant, and we were so excited we ended up taking six suitcases for a seven-day trip! At the airport, in the international terminal, we had to take a really long escalator that seemed to go on forever. My new bride had one suitcase as I insisted on carrying the other five, because I was trying to show off as the new husband. *I've got this. No problem. Barely notice the weight.*
I got on the escalator, and my wife got on a couple of steps behind me. Right as we got to the top, one of the five suitcases I was carrying became caught on the side of the escalator. You know, the part of the escalator that's *not* moving. Since I was on the part that *was* moving, the stuck suitcase pulled me backward, and with all that baggage, I immediately lost my balance. I fell down the escalator, knocking over my wife in the process and taking her with me. True story: here we were going on our honeymoon, and we literally went head over heels from the top of this huge escalator all the way to the bottom. *Bump! Bump! Bump!* Since the escalator was going up and we were going down, we kept having more stairs to hit.

I tried to somehow protect my wife and shield her on the way down, which meant my body took the brunt of the fall. I didn't have any hands free to soften the blows. So I ended up lying at the bottom of the escalator, hurt and bruised and literally bleeding! That's how the very first day of our marriage started.

What I didn't realize then, but soon would learn, was that my fall provided a pretty good preview of what was going to happen in my marriage. You see, I carried a lot of baggage into our marriage. It was baggage I had built up and accumulated throughout my years of dating. Because, just like the way I shopped, I had gone about dating all wrong. I dated for fun. I dated too early. I dated the wrong people, the wrong way, and for the wrong reasons. And though it took about a year after our wedding before we hit a snag, eventually that baggage caught up with me. When it did, it left our marriage, figuratively speaking, bleeding and bruised down at the bottom of the escalator. It took a long time, a lot of work, and a lot of grace to fully repair the damage and lead to the truly healthy marriage we enjoy today.

Knowing what I know now, I definitely wish I had dated differently. If I could have a do-over on my dating years, I would try to avoid creating all that unnecessary baggage.

Dating with an eye toward marriage changes not just when you date and who you date but also how you date. Since the end goal is marriage, you want to do things in dating that will set you up for success in your future marriage—whether that's with the person you're dating currently or with someone else in the future if it doesn't work out with this person. That means having healthy boundaries in dating and not crossing inappropriate lines physically or emotionally. You want to treat them well even if you break up with them, and thereby avoid having any angry exes show up at your wedding.

It also means using your single time wisely. If you are not ready to date, or are not currently dating for whatever reason, that doesn't mean you're stuck waiting passively. You can do yourself and your future spouse a big favor by working to unpack some of your baggage so you won't have to carry it with you into marriage. As I've often said, there are no married people problems—just single people problems carried into marriage.

Where I'm Coming From

If it's not clear already, I'm not telling you these things as some holier-than-thou pastor, asking you to be more like me. It would probably be more accurate to say that I'm asking you to be *less* like me, or at least less like I was during most of the time I was dating. If you feel like you've already made mistakes in dating, know that I made those mistakes too. I badly messed things up. I hurt myself and others in the process. In fact, for one or two girlfriends, I was probably their biggest mistake. That's not a joke. It's quite possible that the worst decision they've ever made in their lives was agreeing to date me. I've had to deal with that fact and seek forgiveness where I could.

I missed it. I listened to the world—culture, movies, TV shows. I loved dating as a sport—the thrill, the feeling of newness, what I could get someone to do, and how far I could get them to go. Honestly, I even in some sick kind of way loved wondering if I'd ever get married, or if anyone would ever love me enough in that way.

What I didn't realize was that, all the while, I was already loved. Despite my faults and my flaws, I was already accepted by One who was perfect. I sought affirmation and adventure and meaning in the dating game, and all the while that was just a secondary narrative to a bigger story I was called to be part of. Our earthly romantic relationships are supposed to be a reflection of, or a peek into, our eternal relationship with our Savior.[f] But I treated dating as something else entirely, selfishly loving myself rather than selflessly loving the person I was with.

f. Ephesians 5:21–33, especially verse 32; also Revelation 19:6–9.

I realize you may look at me now and say, "Hey, man, it worked out for you." In one sense, you're right. I'm married, and married well. In fact, I married far better than I deserve, to the godliest woman I know. We've been married for sixteen years now, and about fourteen of those years have been great. But there were a couple of years in there that were pure misery, and it was all a direct result of the mistakes I'd made when dating. The fact that it eventually worked out for me is fully due to God being massively merciful and gracious in my life. It would be a really poor strategy to try to replicate that. Instead, things will go better if you can learn from the mistakes of others and avoid making them in your own life.

When I look at this generation of young singles in the church today, I can't help but think that if everyone just got *this* right—if people put their selfish desires aside and began to pursue God's desires for each other, and pursued each other the way God desires—that change would be amazing and powerful. There would be a revival. There would be a great awakening. Single people would live on mission, godly marriages would be formed, disciples would be made in the home. Christianity would spread like wildfire in a culture that has been growing cold to it. We could change a generation—and change the world—just by changing the way we date.

2

Singleness Is a Problem to Be Fixed

THE LIE: being single is a waiting period for something better.

THE TRUTH: something better is waiting for you right now.

I love gifts. Not just receiving gifts—I imagine everybody likes that—but also buying and giving gifts. It's one of my love languages.[1]

One year at Christmastime, we had our staff Christmas party at my house, and I wanted to get gifts for everyone on my staff. But instead of getting specific gifts for specific people, I arranged for us to play that game where everyone draws a number and then picks a gift to unwrap in turn, and if you like someone else's gift you have the chance to steal it from them (and then they can replace it by either unwrapping another gift or stealing from someone else). There are many different versions of the game with different names. Sometimes the gifts are things people actually want, and sometimes they are gag gifts or "white elephant" gifts. In the version we played at my house, I bought both kinds of gifts: some that people would really want and some that no one would want.

You've probably played this game yourself, so you know how it goes. With each gift opened, there's this internal evaluation, where the person asks themselves, *Am I going to use this gift, or do I want to lose this gift?* If it's a gift you want to keep, then the hope is that no one will steal it. There are different strategies you can use to try to keep someone from stealing it. You might try to hide the gift, keeping it out of sight and out of mind, so that people just forget about it. Or I've seen people do this kind of reverse sales talk, where they really downplay the gift and insinuate that it's not any good so that no one else will want it (even though they really like it themselves).

On the other hand, if you *don't* like a gift you've unwrapped, then your only hope is that someone else *will* like the gift so that they'll steal it from you, allowing you to choose another one. In that case, you really try to sell the gift; you talk up how great it is, even though you don't think it's that great yourself.

In this particular case, to make things more interesting, I included one particular gift I was sure no one would want. It was a piece of inflatable Christmas yard art: a 7.5-foot-tall inflatable nutcracker. But not just any nutcracker. No, this was a redneck nutcracker. It had a beer belly hanging out of its sleeveless shirt, a snowflake tattoo, missing teeth, a trucker hat, and of course a can of beer in its hand. And the rule for this particular gift was that, if you received it, there was a consequence tied to it. You had to keep it up at your house, prominently displayed for all the world to see, all the way through Christmas—and New Year's—and all of January. It couldn't come down until February!

I told everyone about the redneck nutcracker up front, explaining what the consequences would be if that's the gift they opened. If you opened it, you were stuck with it—no trading. Nobody wanted to receive that gift. I could see them get kind of nervous every time they unwrapped a gift, because they were afraid it might be the redneck nutcracker. In fact, some people were more likely to steal an unwrapped gift from someone else, even if they didn't necessarily want the gift, just because it meant they knew what they'd be getting and wouldn't run the risk of unwrapping the redneck nutcracker.

I tell that story because we're about to discuss something Scripture calls a gift but which most people treat as a gift they really don't want. It's the one gift they desperately don't want to be stuck with. And I'm here to tell you that's based on a wrong understanding of the gift. It truly is a gift from God, but it's one that most people end up wasting. I want you to use the gift, not just try to lose the gift.

The Gift Nobody Wants

The gift I'm talking about is the gift of singleness.

If you grew up in church, as I did, or if you've spent a lot of time there (or a lot of time in the Scriptures), you've probably heard the term "gift of singleness" at some point. (Insert eyeroll here.) It comes primarily from 1 Corinthians

7:7, where the apostle Paul said, "I wish that all of you were as I am. But each of you has your own gift from God; one has this gift, another has that." In context, he's talking about singleness and marriage, and since Paul himself was single (he says so in the very next verse), he's saying that he wishes everyone was single like him. But, as he puts it, some people have the gift of singleness and some have other gifts instead. If you're like most single people I've met, you're probably hoping you *don't* have the gift of singleness. You're like, *Does this "gift" come with a receipt? Maybe I can still exchange it.* Or you're in full-on sales mode, hoping someone will steal it from you.

That's because there's a common myth today that singleness is a problem to be fixed. As in, *I'm single, but I don't want to be, and the solution is to date and/or get married. Like, now. As soon as possible. Because as long as I remain single, I'm living in this problem.*

This myth says that being single is an unnatural state, and that single people are not fully whole or healthy until they find someone else to give their lives meaning. It's the whole "You complete me" mentality, which is just bad Hollywood theology.[a] Singleness is seen as this waiting period, and life only truly begins once you get married. It's like you're stuck in a holding pattern, waiting to take off and take flight as a fully realized, no-longer-single adult.

From what I've seen, this idea that singleness is a problem to be fixed actually appears to be more common among Christians—the very people for whom "the gift of singleness" is meant to apply.

a. "You complete me" is a phrase popularized by the 1996 Tom Cruise film *Jerry Maguire*, and man do I feel old if I now have to explain that to people.

Or maybe you *do* see singleness as a gift, but not at all in the way God intended. You see it as a chance to date around, to jack with people's hearts and pursue physical pleasure with as many people as you can. In that case, you're not using the gift of singleness, you're abusing it. And you're going directly against what 1 Corinthians 7, and the rest of the Bible, has to say about singleness and marriage. In fact, the gift of singleness doesn't have to do with dating at all. It's not "the gift of dating." Dating is not a gift from God, because God didn't create dating; as I've covered, it was invented by modern culture. But God did create singleness, and marriage, and both can be gifts from him.

Do You Have the Gift of Singleness?

To overcome these myths and misconceptions, we need to understand what the gift of singleness really means. So, let's unwrap that gift.

I know the question many of you are asking is, How do I know if I have the gift of singleness? Luckily, I can tell you right now, without a doubt, the answer to that question. (Knowing this alone is worth whatever you paid for this book.) I've created a quiz you can use to determine whether you have the gift of singleness. It's a really simple quiz. In fact, it's only one question. Are you ready? (That's not the question; I'm just asking if you're ready.) Here's the question:

Are you single today?

Here's how you score the quiz. If you answered no, as in "No, I'm married," then you officially don't have the gift of singleness. Sorry. But if you answered yes, as in "Yes, I am single right at this moment," then congratulations! You have the gift of singleness.

Whoa, now, you may be thinking. *Did you just say that I'll be single forever? Don't you put that evil on me, Ricky Bobby!*[b]

No, I did not just say you will be single forever. At least, I'm not saying that yet.

You see, there are a couple of different takes on what the gift of singleness means. And they're both correct, by the way; they just apply to different people or different situations. For some people, it is a spiritual gift that enables them to remain single for life. It's a gift because it allows those people to focus on serving God without being distracted by the need to take care of a spouse and kids. Paul also talks about this in 1 Corinthians 7, especially in verses 32–35.[c] It's sometimes called the gift of celibacy, because the Bible reserves sex for marriage,[d] and so remaining unmarried would mean remaining celibate.

Now, if being single for life is literally your greatest fear, ranking ahead of snakes and sharks and creepy clowns, then it's pretty safe to say that you don't have that spiritual gift. (Or at least not right now. People can change, and gifts can change over time.) Jesus also talked about this gift in

b. This *Talladega Nights: The Ballad of Ricky Bobby* reference is brought to you by Jackhawk Knives.

c. 1 Corinthians 7:32–35: "I would like you to be free from concern. An unmarried man is concerned about the Lord's affairs—how he can please the Lord. But a married man is concerned about the affairs of this world—how he can please his wife—and his interests are divided. An unmarried woman or virgin is concerned about the Lord's affairs: Her aim is to be devoted to the Lord in both body and spirit. But a married woman is concerned about the affairs of this world—how she can please her husband. I am saying this for your own good, not to restrict you, but that you may live in a right way in undivided devotion to the Lord."

d. Much more on that later.

Matthew 19:10–12.[e] He said there are eunuchs (people who physically cannot have sex) and "those who choose to live like eunuchs for the sake of the kingdom of heaven." Note the word *choose*. We have free will. In practice, the gift of celibacy is probably the ability to not be that concerned about getting married or having sex, so that you can freely choose to live life that way.

But even if you don't have the spiritual gift of staying single for life, you're still single right now. And that means you have the same benefits of being able to serve God without the distractions of having to take care of a family. You may not have that gift in the future, but you have it right now. And believe me, it's a valuable gift. If you're single today, you will want to learn how to use this gift immediately.

God's Gifts Are Always Good

I remember another Christmas gift exchange, this time with my wife's extended family. The rules were similar, only no redneck nutcracker. (I know, boring!) There was a $20 spending limit. At this one, my brother-in-law chose a small wrapped package from his uncle. He opened it up, and inside was a plastic stopwatch. It didn't seem like a very good gift, because he didn't have any use for a stopwatch. Even if he needed to time something, we all have smartphones, and

e. Matthew 19:10–12: "The disciples said to him, 'If this is the situation between a husband and wife, it is better not to marry.' Jesus replied, 'Not everyone can accept this word, but only those to whom it has been given. For there are eunuchs who were born that way, and there are eunuchs who have been made eunuchs by others—and there are those who choose to live like eunuchs for the sake of the kingdom of heaven. The one who can accept this should accept it.'"

they have stopwatches built in. But, on top of that, it didn't work. It was a broken stopwatch. My brother-in-law was like, *What am I supposed to do with this?* He didn't want the gift. But then I overheard his uncle say something about it being valuable. It didn't look valuable; it looked like a broken plastic stopwatch.

I told my brother-in-law, "Hey, I think maybe it's worth something." And he said, "Do you want it?" He didn't know what to do with it, and just wanted to be rid of the thing. So I said, "Sure, I'll take it." He didn't even want to trade gifts; he just gave it to me.

But why would I want it? I also didn't need a broken stopwatch. But I'd realized an important fact. I knew that my brother-in-law's uncle loved him. He cared for his family. And because of that, I knew he wouldn't just offer a piece of trash as a gift to those he loved. His uncle would want to give good gifts. And if he gifted a stopwatch that didn't work, it had to be for a reason.

I trusted that the gift was good because I knew the person giving it, and knew he loved the person he was giving it to. And here we're just talking about an imperfect uncle giving a gift to his nephew. When you have a perfect Father—God—handing out gifts to his children, you can trust that he is going to give good gifts. As Jesus described in Matthew 7:9–11,

> Which of you, if your son asks for bread, will give him a stone? Or if he asks for a fish, will give him a snake? If you, then, though you are evil, know how to give good gifts to your children, how much more will your Father in heaven give good gifts to those who ask him!

When I got home, I looked up the stopwatch on eBay. I quickly saw that this type of stopwatch, even in its current condition, was worth about $150 (way over the $20 limit!), and so I sold it. It was worth something—quite a bit, actually—and my brother-in-law just didn't realize it. He didn't know what to do with it. If he had kept the gift, it would have been wasted—he would have probably thrown it away or kept it in a junk drawer or something.

People waste gifts because they either don't realize their value or don't know how to use them. If God gives you a gift, you know it is going to be valuable. The question is, How are you going to use it? If you are single, there's a good chance you have a gift that you're wasting.

Using Your Gift

You will never be more uninhibited, more available, and more ready to serve God than you are right now as a single person. You'll never have more time or fewer responsibilities. You'll never have more freedom or a greater opportunity to take chances and risk something for the gospel.

I know some of you will doubt that. You'll say, "No, JP, you don't understand how busy I am. I have no free time, and no margin to do anything else. I have too many responsibilities already." And as you say that, all my married friends are over here shaking their heads and laughing. Because they know the truth. They were single once too. They've seen both sides. I don't have to convince them that these are the benefits of being single. If I was writing this to married people, it would be a pretty short chapter. They already know.

When you're married, you add another person to the calculations. And when you have kids, the math just multiplies. Your time and your resources are no longer your own. You have other mouths to feed, other schedules to work around, and other people who deserve your time and attention. You can't go and risk your life or your livelihood without considering the life-altering consequences it would have on the people under your care, those whom you care for the most. You're not as free.

I don't say this to insinuate that marriage is a drag, because that's not true, either. Marriage can be amazing. But singleness can be amazing too. They can both be equally good gifts. It just depends on how you use them.

As a married person with kids, my main ministry opportunity is my family. I know; I'm a full-time pastor, so that might sound weird. But it's true. I still spend more hours at home than I do at work, and I have a much greater impact on the disciples I'm making at home. That's my most effective way to make an impact on God's kingdom. It's good, and I'm not complaining. But when I was single, I had so many more opportunities to make a difference with more people.

I'm not sad that I'm no longer single, but I am kind of sad I didn't use my single days more effectively. If I could go back in time to when I was single—not to fantasize but just to say if I could choose today how to spend my time as a single person—there are things I would do dramatically differently.

For starters, I would take an international trip at least once a year to bring the gospel to the dark places of this earth. I might use all of my vacation days doing exactly that. I would also see my workplace as a mission field. When I was single, I worked in the secular business world, which means I had far more opportunities to share the gospel with coworkers. (It turns out, now that I work in a church, that my coworkers tend to already be Christians. So you probably have a greater opportunity to make a difference in that way than I do.) I would share the gospel so much that I would risk losing my job, because I didn't have anyone else to support and could afford to risk that. I would want to be a light in the dark place that can be corporate America.

I would belong to a church. I would become a member there. I would serve there. I would give there. I would come under the authority of the elders there, and I would ask them to help me find out what gifts the Lord has entrusted me with so that I could unleash those gifts for the kingdom. Because I want to make a difference. I want my life to count for something.

I would find like-minded believers to live in community with. Some of us would literally live together, as roommates, so that we could save money and have more resources available to travel the world and to contribute to world-changing causes. We'd constantly be there for each other, and we'd experience this adventure together.

If I were single again, I would get trained. I would use my time to become biblically literate. I would learn the Scriptures. I would listen to sermons and download the podcasts of great Bible teachers to get an education (for free!) and know God's Word through and through. I'd learn how to apply that knowledge so I could go into any situation and know how to bring about the peace and healing and fullness of life God desires for his people.

I would process all decisions in regard to how they would bring glory to God, and how they could have an eternal impact on myself and others. I would ask him constantly, "Lord, how do you want to use my life? What do you want to do through me? I believe you want to do incredible things today. I know that 'the eyes of the LORD range throughout the earth to strengthen those whose hearts are fully committed to him' (2 Chron. 16:9). I pray that you would find me, so that you might use me to change this place."

That's what I would do, if I were single again.

But for you, there's no "if." It's not wishful thinking, requiring some impossible time-travel device. If you're single, you can just start doing all of those things *right now*. This very minute. There's nothing stopping you. Even finishing this chapter can wait.

That's how you use the gift of singleness. Not by playing games or playing the field. Not by twiddling your thumbs and waiting for Mr. or Ms. Right to "complete" you so that life can finally begin. You can start living a full life now.

Single for Good

I know some people who are doing awesome at this. As an example, I have one friend, Shannon, who for a number of years volunteered some of her time to help lead ministry behind the scenes at The Porch. She and a few other people would meet together with me to examine the Scriptures and help plan each week's message.

At one point, I hadn't seen her around for a couple of months. So when she eventually showed back up at our weekly meeting, I asked her how she was doing, and mentioned that I hadn't seen her around in a while. She replied, "I know, man. I've been traveling. Seven weeks, six different places, six different airports, three different countries." "Oh, really?" I said. "Tell me all about it." She had magnificent stories of how God was working through her, and how she was teaching people and leading ministry and discipling young adults all over the world. Then and now, she consistently does the things some of you only dream about doing. Why? Because she's using her singleness.

And you know what's crazy? Some of you probably feel sorry for her, just based on the fact that she's in her forties and is still single. The reality is, she should feel sorry for *you* because you're wasting your singleness. While you see your relationship status as a problem and are focused only on losing your singleness, Shannon is out there using her singleness every day. She's not distracted by a husband or by desperation for one. Her attitude is, *Hey, if God gives me a husband, great. If he entrusts me with that, awesome. But until then I'm single, and I'll leverage the gifts he's given me.*

I have no way of knowing whether she'll ever get married, just like I don't know if you'll ever get married. Statistically, most of you will. Even though the percentages for marriage are down, and people are getting married later in life, a large majority of people will eventually get married. *But if you don't*, because some of you won't, that doesn't mean you've lost out on the game of life. The only way you miss out is if you waste the gifts you've been given, whether they include singleness or marriage.

The apostle Paul, the greatest missionary to ever live, was single, and he said it was good: "I wish you were as I am."[f] You know who else was single? Jesus. Literally the most

---

f. 1 Corinthians 7:7, again.

eligible bachelor on the planet. Right? I've heard people joke about how they're "dating Jesus." But Jesus didn't date. He lived to be thirty-three years old, single, in a culture where people typically got married in their teens.[2] And to be clear, Jesus could have gotten married if he wanted to. He was without sin, but getting married is not a sin.[g] Yet he chose not to take a wife because he was on a mission, and he didn't want that distraction of marriage. Mother Teresa was also single for life. She had a pretty big impact. The vast majority of people with "Saint" in front of their names: also single.[3] All sorts of people have lived the very fullest of lives and yet did so without getting married.

Something else that's interesting: in heaven, we will all be single. We'll literally be single forever. I know; it's weird to think about, because I'm married right now. But somehow, Monica and I won't be married in heaven, according to Matthew 22:30 and other verses.[h] So, in heaven, which is a perfect paradise, everyone will be single (or married to Jesus, depending on how you look at it).[i]

If you desire to get married, I hope you will. You probably will. Hopefully this book can help. But while you are single, whether that's for a season or for the rest of your life, know that you're not "less than." You're not incomplete. Your singleness is not a problem to be fixed; it's a gift to be used to live life more fully.

g. 1 Corinthians 7:28: "But if you do marry, you have not sinned."
h. Matthew 22:30: "At the resurrection people will neither marry nor be given in marriage; they will be like the angels in heaven." See also Mark 12:25 and Luke 20:34–36.
i. See Revelation 19:7–8 and 21:9–10, as well as 2 Corinthians 11:2. Like I said, it depends on how you look at it.

PART 2

who we date

3

The One

THE LIE: you have to find the one person, made just
for you, who was created around the same time you
were—and they are out there, lost in the world of
eight billion people.

THE TRUTH: there are many people you can choose from,
and really just a few places to look for them.

Once upon a time, in the magical land of Waco, Texas. . . .

Wait, that doesn't sound right. Sorry, this must be a different kind of story. Let me start over.

A number of years ago—I lose track of exactly how long it has been—while living in Waco, I met a beautiful princess named Monica. . . .

Oh, sorry, I did it again. This isn't a fairy tale. This is how my wife and I ended up together in real life.

To be honest, what really happened is I met a guy named Matt, and we became best friends. It just so happened he had a sister named Monica, and I couldn't help but notice she was really cute.

Did I know then that she was the perfect one for me? No. Actually, from the very first second I laid eyes on her, I knew she was *not* perfect for me. Why do I say that? Simply because while I'm 6'7" tall, she's only 5'3". That's not a perfect height differential.

Besides that minor physical difference, we've learned there are many other ways in which we are not truly perfect for each other. We have different interests. For example, while I like motorcycles, guns, and mixed martial arts, she likes—well, *not* motorcycles, guns, or MMA. We have different temperaments. She's the gentlest, most patient person you'll ever meet in your life, whereas my tendency is to be blunt and confront. We're just different people, in ways that do not always seem complementary. In fact, after sixteen years of marriage, we've each changed enough that you could say that I'm a different person than the guy Monica married, and Monica is a different person now than the girl that I married.

If you were to ask me whether there was someone out there who is a better match for Monica than I am, the answer would be a resounding yes. There are probably a lot of men who would be a better match for her, just like there are probably lots of women who would be a better match for me. I mean, with almost eight billion people on the planet, it seems certain that there would be hundreds, or thousands, or even hundreds of thousands of people who would be more compatible with each of us.

Some of you may have your mind blown right now. "Wait, JP, are you saying you married the wrong person?"

No, I'm absolutely not saying that. Monica is the one for me. But she's "the one" because I married her. Because I made a decision, and stood in front of God and family and committed to be her husband, for better or worse, no matter what. It doesn't sound like a fairy tale because it's not a fairy tale. It's real life. And you'll fare much better in dating and marriage if you live in reality rather than in a fairy tale.

Finding "the One"

Too many people approach dating with the idea that it's all about finding "the one." That there is this one person out there who is right for you, and finding them is the entire point of the plot. Once you find that person, you're done. You've won. Because this person is perfect. Not truly perfect—we all know that nobody is perfect—but this person is perfect *for you*, just as you are perfect for them. They are your "soul mate." And because of this "match made in heaven," once you do find each other, everything will work out perfectly. The hard work is finding each other; once you find them, the relationship will be easy, because it's a perfect fit. You'll get married and never have conflict and always make each other happy.

And I'm here to tell you this is a fairy tale. It's a myth. In fact, the term *soul mate* is literally from a myth: the concept comes from an ancient story that claimed humans originally had four arms, four legs, and two faces. In this story, the mythical god Zeus cut each person in half, creating the two-legged men and women we know today—but each with only half a soul. Since each person was only one half of a whole, they were literally incomplete unless or until they found the one person on earth who was their other half—their "soul mate" who had the other half of their soul.[1] So when you talk about finding your "soul mate," you might as well be saying "Release the Kraken!"[a]—they are both myths, and are both equally unlikely to happen.

So if you're looking for your "soul mate," or "the one," or your "twin flame," or whatever you want to call it, and you define that as being the one person on the planet who is perfect for you—you'll never find them. They don't exist. They're off riding unicorns with Bigfoot.

You should be thankful for this. Although it may seem less magical or romantic, it is more hopeful. Finding "the one" can feel like a desperately difficult search—because it is. One NASA scientist ran the numbers and determined that, if "soul mates" were real, only one person out of *ten thousand* would find their mate over the course of a lifetime.[2] And that was using the most optimistic assumptions. That's the reality of trying to find "the one." But in reality, there isn't just one. Instead, there are many "ones" available who would make a great mate for you. If you know how and where to look, the odds of finding one of the many are actually quite high.

First, though, you have to stop searching for "the one." Having this common mindset leads to all kinds of problems in dating and in marriage.

Overlooking Good Options

One problem with looking for "the one" is that it can keep you single far longer than you need to be—maybe forever. Obviously, if you're looking for someone who doesn't exist,

a. A command spoken by Zeus in *Clash of the Titans*, both the 1981 and 2010 versions of the film.

you're going to have a really hard time finding them. And when you do meet someone, even a great someone who could make a wonderful spouse, any tiny flaw or minor difference of opinion may be seen as proof that they're not "the one" for you.

Or you may think there is some kind of magical spark that occurs when you meet the right person, and you each immediately know you are meant to be together. So you don't even bother to get to know someone, or you quickly put them into the "friend zone," because you didn't sense any instant connection.

The fact is, you've almost certainly met multiple people who could have been a wonderful match for you, but you never gave them a chance because you were looking for some kind of mystical sign that will never come—or, if it did come, would not be trustworthy.

Ignoring Red Flags

Besides keeping you out of a relationship, the idea of "the one" can also keep you in the wrong relationship too long. This happens whenever you become convinced you have found "the one" and start dating them. Because you think they are "the one," the relationship likely becomes very serious very quickly. But then red flags start to appear. Maybe this person has vastly different beliefs than you do. Maybe they push you to go too far physically, or they cheat on you with someone else. Maybe they even become abusive (although you refuse to call it that). If you believe from the start that they are "the one," the *only* one, the person you are destined to be with for life, then you are vastly more likely to overlook such things. You'll ignore your friends and family when they all say that your boyfriend or girlfriend is no good for you and you should break up with them. After all, how can you break up if you're meant to be together? And if you leave the only one for you, doesn't that mean there would be no one left? If you say goodbye to "the one," doesn't that mean you'll now be single forever?

The real answer to those questions, of course, is that there is no magical "one," and so you are free to break up with (and definitely should break up with) anyone you are dating who proves they would not make a good spouse. But believing in this "soul mate" fairy tale can keep you stuck in some very bad dating relationships and lead to a very un-fairy-tale ending. In those situations, the best-case scenario is that you do eventually come to your senses and choose to break up (or get broken up with), but at the cost of lost time, pain, disappointment, and likely some other consequences as well. And that's the best-case scenario.

Setting Unrealistic Expectations

The idea of "the one" can also cause you to be unhappy in a good relationship due to the unrealistic expectations it creates. There's actually been research about this problem, based on the effects of watching romantic comedies. Psychologists found that the idea of "the one," which is a prevalent theme in rom-coms, causes people to think that relationships should be easy.[3] For example, they found that people believed that their spouse or "soul mate" should be able to know what they were thinking without having to say it out loud. This led to communication problems in their relationships, since people basically didn't communicate at all and then got upset when the other person couldn't read their minds. People also believed that once they found the "right" person, a long-term relationship with them should be easy and not require ongoing work.

This makes sense in a rom-com or Disney princess world, since those movies (spoiler alert) almost always end at the *beginning* of the real relationship. They end with a wedding, or an engagement, or simply the two leads kissing for the very first time. That's the end of the story. The story is about finding "the one," which in Hollywood is the dramatic part that requires overcoming obstacles. It's implied, or outright stated, that couples then live "happily ever after," with no ongoing conflicts or drama worth making a romantic movie about. The impression people get is that the hard part's over, when in reality it's the relationship that requires sacrifice and work.

The result, then, is that people get dissatisfied with a real, lifelong relationship. When they realize their spouse isn't perfect, marriage takes work to be successful, and the initial spark fades away, they see this as evidence that the person they married is not "the one" after all, because if they were "the one," the relationship would be easy and exciting and perfect. They become disillusioned and lose interest. And then, when someone new comes along and they again feel that initial excitement, they think that surely *this person* is "the one." They believe they made a mistake the first time and chose the wrong person. So they have an affair and/or get a divorce so they can pursue this new "soul mate."

And then they go through the same process of disillusionment with the new person, who, it turns out, is *also* not perfect. Wash, rinse, repeat. This explains not only the overall divorce rate but also the fact that second and third marriages are even *more* likely to end in divorce.[4] Again, if you're stuck on looking for the magical "one," you are looking for something that doesn't exist.

So belief in a "soul mate" can end up ruining a relationship, because you always end up searching for something else. And even *that* sad process gets romanticized by Hollywood. Just think of how many movies revolve around the concept of a girl (or occasionally a guy) who is engaged to or seriously dating one person but then leaves them for someone else because this other person is "the one."[b] We've essentially redefined cheating as "romance."

Real romance means making a commitment and then, once you are committed, sticking to it. It takes work, because all relationships take work. My relationship with my own kids takes work. Even my relationship with my truck takes work, requiring regular maintenance and the occasional major repair. It may not be magic, but it does keep everything running smoothly.

The One for You

As I said at the outset, my wife and I are not perfect for each other. We're not long-lost "soul mates" who finally found each other and became complete. There are surely men out

b. I did think about it, and here's a very partial list: *The Notebook*; *The Family Stone*; *The Sound of Music*; *The Wedding Singer*; *The Wedding Planner*; *The Runaway Bride*; *The Princess Bride*; *Enchanted* (twice); *Titanic*; *You've Got Mail*; *Sleepless in Seattle*; *Notting Hill* (maybe); *Sweet Home Alabama* (definitely); *Definitely, Maybe*; *Spaceballs*; and *Twister*. Note that in most cases the ditched significant other is actually a pretty decent guy (or girl). With the exception of a few villains (who deserve to get dumped), they are typically successful, attractive, and reliable. They're just not considered exciting or romantic.

there who would be more compatible or better suited for her than I am, and there are probably other women out there who could at least tolerate me.

However, we're not looking for those people. We're never going to search for anybody else. We don't need to find anyone else. We married each other, and so we belong to each other for the rest of this life. In that very real way, we are "the one" for each other—not because of some predestined magical or mystical reason but because we choose to be. And even when one of us is imperfect or fails—because everyone is imperfect and everyone fails—we know we will *still* be there for each other and will never give up on each other or leave for someone else.

You see, when you marry someone, they do become "the one." They're the one you've committed to love for the rest of your life. The Bible even says that the two of you together become one (Mark 10:7–8). And they will still be the one when they gain weight, lose weight, lose their job, get cancer, or make mistakes.

It's not magical, but that's what makes it wonderful. It means you're accepted and loved and secure in your relationship despite your flaws. It means you'll always pursue each other and work to reconcile any disagreements, because that's what you've taken a covenant[c] vow to do.

In other words, it sounds a lot like our relationship with Christ.

---

c. Marriage is a covenant, which is different from a contract. In a contract, both sides agree to fulfill their parts of a deal. If either party fails to fulfill their side of the bargain, then they have "broken" the contract and the agreement is no longer in effect. With a covenant, though, you agree to fulfill the terms even if the other person fails to do what they said they would do. That's why marriage vows say "for better or worse," and "until death do us part."

If you're looking for a "soul mate," what you're really looking for is Jesus. He actually is perfect, and is the only one who can truly satisfy your soul.

Love Jesus first, with all your heart, and then find someone who loves him just as much and marry that person. Or, if you don't marry, you'll still be OK—because you're not looking for someone else to make you complete.

4

Love at First Sight

THE LIE: physical attraction is ultimate.

THE TRUTH: physical qualities ultimately won't last, but you can look for character that will.

I remember when my oldest daughter, Presley, entered kindergarten and began experiencing all the social interactions of school. One day, midway through the year, I picked her up from school, and on the drive home she started talking about this friend of hers. It was some kid named Avery whom I'd never met. "Daddy, do you know what infinity means? Avery taught me what infinity means." She went on and on about Avery: Avery taught me this, Avery taught me that.

I was happy that she was making friends, so I was like, "Oh, cool. How long have you been friends with her?"

She said, "No, Daddy, Avery is a boy."

Oh man. My protective dad instincts kicked in, and I started getting nervous. "Oh, OK. So . . . sounds like y'all talk a lot. Is . . . is Avery your boyfriend?"

"No."

Something about the way she said that made me wonder. So I asked, "Presley, do you have a boyfriend?"

"Yes."

Now I could hardly breathe. Who was this five-year-old Romeo whom I was already sure would never be good enough for my daughter?

Catching my breath, I asked her, "What's your boyfriend's name?"

Surprisingly, she had to think about this for a second. "I don't know his name," she finally replied.

It's funny, when you're five years old, not to realize that, in a relationship, knowing the other person's name is *kind of* important. That's a pretty basic level of knowing someone.

It's a bit less funny when you're twenty-five years old, or even thirty-five years old, and you still don't know what is important in relationships. When you can still make decisions about somebody—yes or no, I want to date you or not—without even knowing the person's name.

I'm talking about the concept of "love at first sight," and, more broadly, just the overall idea that love is based on looks.

Now, you may already be objecting that physical attractiveness isn't the *only* thing you consider when you contemplate dating someone. But I'm willing to bet it's the first thing you consider, as well as the factor that carries the most weight. (That may not be true for everyone, but if I made that bet with one hundred people, I'd probably win ninety times and more than cover the cost of the losses.)

The thing you need to realize is that physical attractiveness is not all that important. It is by far the most overrated aspect of dating relationships. *By far.*

Beauty Is Fleeting

The Bible speaks directly to this. Proverbs 31:30 says, "Charm is deceptive, and beauty is fleeting; but a woman who fears the LORD is to be praised."

Although this verse is talking about a woman, this "beauty is fleeting" concept holds true for both women and men. We're all getting older, and it shows. Our faces and our bodies change. It's just basic biology. As I write this, I'm not even forty yet (though I'm getting close), and even though I hit the gym weekly, it is certainly happening to me!

Think about it: when's the last time you were physically attracted to an eighty-year-old? Yet, once upon a time, a lot of those eighty-year-olds were drop-dead gorgeous. Your grandparents might have been hot. That's weird, I know. But it's true.

I happened to read an article online that was talking about beauty, and it mentioned the names of several actresses who, according to the article, were among the most beautiful people in Hollywood. And I was confused. Although I recognized the names and knew they were well-respected actresses, they were also kind of, well, old. They might look OK for their age, but I didn't think they would make anyone's list of the most beautiful people. Then I looked at the date of the article and realized it had been written a few decades ago and had been posted online as part of a newspaper archive. I looked up the movies these actresses had been in around that time and saw that, sure enough, they had been attractive then. They were the beautiful stars other girls would have dreamed about being and guys would have dreamed about dating. But now some of them are better known for playing the roles of—I kid you not—witches. Wrinkled, grumpy old witches.

What happened? They got older. And as they got older, they were no longer asked to play the romantic lead, because Hollywood doesn't look at romance that way. When pop culture shows us romance, we're almost always watching people in their prime. But that prime doesn't last.

If you're lucky, it will happen to you one day too. You'll get old. If you're married, your spouse will get old as well. And if their youthful physical beauty was the main reason you married them, that reason for being together will be long gone.

A corollary to this is that if you attract someone with your looks, you will lose them for the same reason. If that's the reason they are interested in you, then they will logically leave you when your looks change or when someone more attractive comes along. If that's the "bait" you actively try to lure them with, through the way you dress or the way you pose in the images you post online, then don't be surprised at the type of fish you catch. Using your body does work, but it works in attracting someone who wants to use your body. And if someone will pick you out and pick you up at first sight, without knowing *anything* about you except for what you look like, they're not really interested in you as a person. They're interested in you as a pretty plaything.

If you choose a mate based on physical beauty, you're investing in a depreciating asset. It's "fleeting," which is literally defined as "passing swiftly" or "vanishing quickly." That's a really bad investment strategy.

Beauty Is Fake

Beauty is fleeting in another way: the very definition of what counts as "beautiful" changes over time. Just like there are fashion trends for clothing, what's considered an attractive body type or facial feature follows trends, with different looks falling in and out of favor with some regularity. We may think of beauty as this unchanging ideal standard, but it's actually a made-up media narrative.

I studied art in college, and if you know your art history, you've likely noticed this at some point yourself. When people from past centuries painted beautiful women,[a] they often portrayed someone who would be considered "plus-sized" by today's standards. According to one sixteenth-century Parisian doctor, the ideal woman should have pale skin and a double chin.[1] Apparently, the more chins, the better. That was hot. Back then, the very concept of tanning or dieting would have been confusing. Why would you try to make yourself uglier?

What was considered ideal varies depending on the century and what is popular at that time. Ancient Greeks valued physical fitness, but they also thought that a unibrow was particularly attractive.[2]

a. I focus on media-driven beauty trends for women, rather than men, throughout this section because, frankly, that's what the media focuses on. There are also beauty trends for men, but they're not nearly as obvious or extreme. And yes, the fact that the weight of this problem falls on women, with very real consequences for women's health and self-esteem, is unfair and sad. Which is why God's Word speaks against it and why I'm arguing against it here.

In the 1920s, with the "flapper" look the trend in fashion, women were considered beautiful if they were rail-thin, with no curves at all.[3] By the 1940s that had changed to the curvy hourglass figure of models like Marilyn Monroe, only to return to the ultra-thin look in the 1960s with "Twiggy," a model nicknamed for her stick-like shape.[4] In the 1980s, it was about fitness. In the 1990s, it was thin again. Today, you see some celebrities with seemingly impossible body shapes being idolized. The prevalence of online pornography has popularized a fake, artificially enhanced look.

The point is, the media—in all the many forms it has taken over the years—is defining for us what "beautiful" means. We're being told what to find attractive. I know that's hard to understand. It feels like something innate inside us—that we are *naturally* attracted to a certain look. But, to a large extent, attraction is taught. It's based on the images you've been fed or that you choose to feed yourself.

There are consequences to all this. Dangerous eating disorders, such as anorexia nervosa, become more common when the trendy body type is thinner.[5] When your own natural look doesn't match up with what is currently on-trend, it can lead to body image issues and low self-esteem—even though you might have been considered ideally beautiful a few decades or centuries ago. Too fat, too thin, too dark, too pale, too anything—at some point, you would have been considered beautiful, and the only thing that's changed is what the media has decided should be fashionable.

So be aware of what you're being told and how you're being sold. Don't let society dictate to you what you should find attractive or whether you are beautiful. Be careful what you're telling yourself and how you're training your eyes with what you look at and what you long for. If you're only attracted to a certain unrealistic type, try feeding your eyes a different diet.

Beauty Can Be a Negative

Beauty is fleeting, beauty is fake, and in some cases beauty can even be a negative.

We all know that life isn't always fair, and one way this is true is that society favors physically beautiful people. People treat them differently. Attractive people are more likely to get the job or make the sale.[6] They tend to make more money than similarly qualified but less attractive co-workers.[7] People perceive them to be smarter, healthier, happier, more trustworthy, and more honest.[8] And that's not even mentioning how much easier it is for them to find a date.

How does that kind of favoritism impact a person? For some people, it would not be a problem. They still work just as hard, are just as humble, and feel just as grateful as someone who does not have such an ever-present advantage. But for most people, I think it does have an impact. Why work hard to develop positive character traits that will last when people will already give you all the attention and adoration you could want just for being pretty? There would have to at least be a temptation to skate by on looks alone.

There's also the question of whether good looks have become an idol in the person's life. Looking good often takes a lot of time and effort: a lot of hours spent in the gym, and a lot of resources put into "outward adornment."[b] There's nothing wrong with being fit, and you are free to dress nicely if you want. But if that's a huge chunk of your life, it doesn't leave much time for developing your "inner self" and the "unfading beauty" that are considered to have "great worth" in 1 Peter 3:3–4. (Also, contrast the "unfading" internal beauty to the "fleeting" external beauty of Proverbs 31:30.)

Plus, I think we like beauty because we equate it with better sex. But is that even true? Studies have found that couples become more satisfied with their sex lives as they get older, which suggests that physical beauty isn't all that important in the bedroom.[9] After all, we are talking about the thing that people usually do with the lights off. That's the irony: you choose someone based on something that carries very little relevance to a successful marriage and which often makes them difficult to be married to.

Beauty can also be a negative for you if it causes you to chase after the wrong people when dating. Outward beauty is a very poor predictor of success in relationships. In fact, it is a *negative* predictor of long-term success, possibly for the exact reasons I've mentioned above. A series of four Harvard studies found that more attractive people were significantly more likely to divorce and less likely to be satisfied with their current romantic relationship.[10] So if you are mostly interested in dating someone just because they are physically attractive, then you are most likely not going to be happy with the outcome.

b. 1 Peter 3:3–4: "Your beauty should not come from outward adornment, such as elaborate hairstyles and the wearing of gold jewelry or fine clothes. Rather, it should be that of your inner self, the unfading beauty of a gentle and quiet spirit, which is of great worth in God's sight."

Asking Out of Your League

A lot of this makes the optimistic assumption you actually *can* get a date with that hot guy or girl you have your eye on. Maybe you can. But for just about everyone, the focus on physical attractiveness makes dating harder than it has to be. For years, one of the most common complaints I've heard from single women is that guys don't ask them out. Yet, at the same time, one of the biggest complaints I've heard from single men is that girls always say no when guys do ask them out. That seemed confusing to me. If women aren't being asked out, then who is telling the guys no? And why would the answer always be no if they are longing for someone to ask them on a date?

Then, after doing a little bit of research, I figured out what is happening. Guys *are* asking girls out, but they are all asking out *the same girls*. They start at the "top" and ask out the "hottest" women. Let's say it's the top 10 percent, just for the sake of discussion. Now, those women get asked out all the time, so they are picky. They have to be; if all of the men are asking out just 10 percent of women, then that 10 percent have to say no to the vast majority of them. As a result, 90 percent of men hear almost nothing but no, leading them to think that's what all women say. Meanwhile, the other 90 percent of women are rarely asked out at all, resulting in their valid complaint about men not asking. Everybody ends up frustrated.

This isn't just a theory; there is some real evidence for it, at least in the world of dating apps. Statistics from several different apps show that a small percentage of its users get the majority of the attention.[11] The stats also show that this is just as true for men as it is for women; women also tend to focus on the "hottest" guys. For some of you, saying that "Guys don't ask me out" really means that *the guys you want* aren't asking you out. You don't even count the ones who do get up the courage to ask but who get turned down because you don't consider them to be worthy.

Part of the problem is that we're constantly consuming content that is filled with beautiful people. Sometimes it's impossibly beautiful people, such as the artificially enhanced bodies of porn stars or movie stars who employ a whole team of people to make sure they look good. We train ourselves to look for physical perfection, even when we don't live up to those standards ourselves. Then, through social media or dating apps, we scroll through a massive number of profile pictures and choose only our physical favorites to focus on. As a result, the whole dating economy is thrown out of whack, with most people getting either rejected or overlooked.

The Economics of Baseball (and Dating)

You may have seen the 2011 movie *Moneyball*, or perhaps read the book it was based on. *Moneyball* tells the real-life story of a major league baseball team that didn't have the money to compete with richer teams. Success came from having the best players, and if a team wasn't able to pay as much as the competition, it wasn't going to get any of them.

But how do you determine who the best players are? At that time in baseball, people would look at specific stats, especially batting average, and assume that players who had the best statistics were the best players overall. Teams would bid top-dollar to get the players with the best batting average. They would *overpay* for a good batting average, because they *overvalued* that particular characteristic in a player. Batting average was a "pretty" stat, always featured prominently on baseball cards and box scores. It was easy to find. What the real-life characters in *Moneyball* realized was that there were other characteristics and statistics that had a bigger impact on whether a player, and therefore a team, would be successful. They had to dig a little deeper to find these other stats; they were buried further down the box score and weren't as obvious as batting average. But because other teams were so focused on batting average, they were undervaluing or simply ignoring players who were actually better at these other, more important statistics. By focusing on the right stats, this one team was able to get *better* players at a *lower* price, enabling them to compete with and beat teams with two or three times their payroll.

What does *Moneyball* and the economics of baseball have to do with dating? As I mentioned, physical attractiveness is far overrated in the world of dating. Nearly everyone tries to date the hot guy or the cute girl. But physical attractiveness has very little actual value when it comes to having a successful, lifelong marriage relationship.

However, there are other attributes that *do* contribute to success in marriage. There are other "stats" that are far more important than looks. But since everyone is focused on physical beauty, the people who maybe aren't the "hottest" prospects, but who actually would make the best spouses, far too often get overlooked. They're out there, waiting for someone like you. And whereas (let's be honest) you probably wouldn't have a shot with the "hot" guy or girl—there's too much competition there—you could actually have a lot of success with the person who doesn't get asked out as much as they deserve. You could finally "win," in dating and in marriage, by focusing on the right characteristics.

A Better Investment Strategy

What characteristics should you focus on? If physical beauty is a depreciating asset, what should you invest in instead? If it doesn't predict success in relationships, what does?

Again, Proverbs 31:30 says that "beauty is fleeting; but a woman who fears the LORD is to be praised." Look for a woman (or a man) who fears the Lord.

What does it mean to fear the Lord? It means following him. It means focusing on eternal things, which are things that truly last. It means striving to see people the way God sees them. In 1 Samuel 16:7, "the LORD said to Samuel, 'Do not consider his appearance or his height, for I have rejected him. The LORD does not look at the things people look at. People look at the outward appearance, but the LORD looks at the heart.'"

Looking at a person's heart takes time. It's not instantly apparent, the way physical beauty can be. It's not "love at first sight." You're probably going to have to get to know the person's name first.

But, although it might take a little bit of time, it's actually not all that hard to look at the heart. All you have to do is look at how they spend their time. Look at what they focus on and what they've ordered their life around. Do they spend more time at the gym or in the Bible? (Or do they spend time in the Bible at the gym? That works too.) Do they love and serve others?ᶜ Are they part of a community of believers,ᵈ and do they submit to their teaching and correction when needed?ᵉ

Most of all, fearing the Lord means obeying his commands. Not perfectly, of course; we all fall short of that.ᶠ But someone who fears the Lord would not willfully and regularly ignore what the Lord has commanded us to do. He or she would not flaunt their disobedience or pretend that sin is no big deal. And when it comes to physical attraction, someone who fears the Lord would not be actively trying to sleep with you outside of marriage. When someone does that, they are quite clearly saying, without even having to use words, that they are not scared of God. They don't really care what he has to say. (Much more on that later.)

Invest in godliness. Learn to value the characteristics that can appreciate over time. Beauty depreciates; that "hot" guy or girl will definitely cool off as they age. But if you choose someone because they are kind, selfless, patient, and wise, they can actually become better at all of those things over time. If you are attracted to godliness, the person you are with can become more attractive as you grow up and grow old together. And I can guarantee those traits will have a bigger impact on your happiness

c. John 13:34–35: "A new command I give you: Love one another. As I have loved you, so you must love one another. By this everyone will know that you are my disciples, if you love one another."

d. Hebrews 10:24–25: "And let us consider how we may spur one another on toward love and good deeds, not giving up meeting together, as some are in the habit of doing, but encouraging one another—and all the more as you see the Day approaching."

e. Hebrews 13:17: "Have confidence in your leaders and submit to their authority, because they keep watch over you as those who must give an account. Do this so that their work will be a joy, not a burden, for that would be of no benefit to you."

f. Romans 3:23: "For all have sinned and fall short of the glory of God."

and the success of your relationship than the way they look right now.

My Trophy Wife

I'm always a little bit self-conscious when talking about this topic because I'm married to someone who is very physically attractive. So, I anticipate the objection: "That's easy for you to say; look who you're married to!"

Yes. It is easy for me to say. And here's why.

After sixteen years of marriage, I know exactly how important Monica's physical beauty is in comparison to her other godly traits. And it really pales in comparison.

When we get into a disagreement, it's not my wife's beauty that helps resolve the conflict and bring peace back to our marriage. When we face a big decision about taking a new job or moving to a new town, it's not her blonde hair and emerald green eyes that bring wisdom into our conversations. When our kids are sick and are projectile vomiting all over the house (and all over us), it doesn't really matter whether she looks good in a bikini right then or not. I don't need a trophy wife by my side; I need someone to go into battle with me.

And that's where you're headed. That's real life. It's not some fairy-tale fantasy where, just because the prince is charming and the princess is young and beautiful, they can fall in love at first sight and live happily ever after. There's a reason fairy tales get remakes rather than sequels: a sequel would have to show what a love based on looks is really like.

Maybe my wife is a trophy; she's certainly a blessing on my life. But it's because of her lasting character, not her temporary looks.

Change Your Standards

Obviously, I'm not saying you *can't* marry someone who's attractive. I did, and I would absolutely marry her again. But I wouldn't marry her again just because she's beautiful. I'd marry her again even if she *wasn't* that attractive, because now I know how important all those other positive traits are.

And I'm not saying you should marry someone you're not attracted to at all. However, attraction goes (or should go) far beyond the physical. Train yourself to be attracted to the things God finds attractive. Those are the things that will last. People ask all the time, "How important are looks?" You must be able to cherish whoever you marry for the rest of their life. If you can't cherish someone who loves Jesus but isn't all that physically attractive, that has much more to say about your spiritual maturity than their looks. You're not yet attracted to what God finds attractive.

Don't lower your standards; change your standards. Instead of saying someone has to be at least a "7" on the imaginary physical attractiveness scale, look for someone who's striving to be a "perfect 10" in terms of godliness.

"A woman who fears the LORD is to be praised." And to be asked out on a date.

5

Love Is a Feeling

THE LIE: you should follow your heart.

THE TRUTH: you should tell your heart what to follow.

OK, so I have another story about my daughter Presley. Sorry, Presley.

When Presley was little, she absolutely loved cats. She was obsessed with them. If you're around toddlers much, you probably know how they can fixate on one thing they really love. Maybe it's bubbles, or trucks, or puppies. Whatever it is, they just become addicted to it, they love it so much. For Presley, that was cats. She *loved* cats.

Unfortunately, the feeling wasn't mutual. Cats *hated* Presley. I mean, they were fine with her at first. When a cat first met Presley, it would treat her the same way it would any other human. (Which is, I suppose, just aloof indifference, because it's a cat.) But then Presley would get ahold of it, and the cat would quickly learn the error of being indifferent to humans. Because when Presley would go to pick it up, she'd pick it up by its fur. Or she'd bend down to give it a hug, but in the process she'd step on its tail. Or she'd grab a kitten (because, after a while, all the adult cats learned to run away from her, but the kittens were too slow) and she'd start tossing it up in the air, saying, "Look, Daddy, it likes to do flips!" And the poor little thing would just be terrified. I'd have to explain to her, "No, baby girl, it doesn't like to do flips. Please stop. I know you don't mean to, but you're actually being kind of cruel to it right now."

You see, although Presley loved cats, she had no idea *how* to love cats. She had all these feelings and emotions toward them, and she didn't know what to do with them.

With people as with pets, emotions aren't enough. A relationship based on feelings will only lead to feelings of hurt. And if your goal is to find love, you'd better understand what "love" is.

What Is Love?

The prevailing wisdom of the world is that love is a feeling, and that dating and marriage are based on these feelings. It's all about the feels. All the feels.

Along with that definition comes the idea that these feelings are out of our control. We talk about "falling in love," which sounds a bit like tripping and falling into a hole. It's a passive action; you fall by accident, and the results of falling down are never all that great. Or you can fall "head over heels," which is even worse: it suggests that you are tumbling out of control in a way sure to leave you bruised and bleeding (see my escalator story in chapter 1 for a vivid mental image, if you need one).

Addicted to Love

Another popular metaphor, especially within music lyrics, is that love is a drug.[a] It's a feeling that gives you a high. A temporary high that leaves you feeling low afterward—until you can get your next (still temporary) fix. You're left constantly chasing after the next high, until you're addicted to the cycle of highs and lows. (This, by the way, perfectly describes much of my dating life before marriage. Looking back now, it was a total waste of time and led to many regrets.)

Public service announcement: love is not a drug. Dating is not a drug. And if you buy into the lyrics and the lies, you're going to end up in a world of hurt.

What do people do with drugs? People use drugs, get addicted to drugs, and get hurt by drugs. What happens when you treat dating as a drug? You use people, you get addicted to people, and then you get hurt by people (and hurt people). And when you get addicted to chasing that feeling, as I did, you eventually have to deal with the withdrawal. When you begin to try to learn how to do dating right, it's going to be painful, because all you know is what's wrong, and you're hooked on it. You're addicted to the drama of it all. If that's you, you've probably already found yourself frustrated with this book. Hang in there.

---

a. Examples include "Your Love Is My Drug" by Ke$ha, "Pusher Love Girl" by Justin Timberlake, "I Love the Way You Lie" by Eminem and Rihanna, and of course the old "Addicted to Love" by Huey Lewis and the News.

Save the Drama

I've heard many people say they don't want drama in dating. It's a common refrain; maybe you've even said it yourself. However, even though you may say you don't want drama, in a way you kind of do. If you're complaining about it, it's only because you've experienced it over and over in your dating relationships. It's what you are used to, and it's all you've ever seen and known. It's the diet you've fed yourself, and it's what you've been entertained by. Television and movies are focused on drama; it is literally the name of the genre. The manic highs and manic lows, breaking up and getting back together again, not being able to decide what you feel or who you love—it all makes for entertaining story lines. It's fun to watch. But it's not that fun to live out.

God wants something better for you than that. But they won't make any movies about it. That's because God is not some unseen audience, watching you suffer for his entertainment. He wants what is best for you, not what is best for ratings. And when a man and a woman commit to each other, sacrificially serve each other, and actively love each other regardless of their temporary feelings, do you know what that is? It's boring. From a dramatic or entertainment standpoint, it doesn't make for must-watch TV. Both people are faithful; there's no change in cast or characters. The inevitable conflicts are resolved quickly. There's no "will they or won't they" tension, because you know they always will. A healthy, godly marriage is not entertaining. It's amazing; it's beautiful; it's an incredible adventure; it's boring. You wouldn't want to watch it, but you do want to live it.

Feelings Are Real, but They're Not Reliable

The problem with defining love as a feeling—which is the root cause of thinking love is out of your control, is a drug, and is a roller coaster of confusion and drama—is that feelings are not reliable. Feelings change, almost by definition. If they didn't change, they wouldn't be feelings; they'd just be who you are.

If your relationship is based solely on feelings, it's guaranteed not to last. You may yo-yo back and forth for a while—you love them, you hate them, you love them again—but eventually the feelings will fade. And if those faded feelings are the basis for your relationship, you'll have no reason to stay together anymore.

Feelings are also not a reliable judge of reality. I may feel that something or someone is right for me, but that feeling doesn't automatically make it true. Facts trump feelings, and the fact is you can feel intensely in love with someone who is incredibly wrong for you. I've seen it happen so many times, and you probably have too. From the outside looking in, it's painfully obvious.

"Why don't you leave him?" "*Because I love him!*"

"Why are you still dating her, after all she's done to you? Can't you see the red flags?" "*Love is blind!*"

Every relationship you've been in was probably defined by feelings. You most likely jumped into a relationship because of how you felt. Likewise, you jumped out of a relationship because of how you felt. It seems in dating, we are ruled by our feelings, but these feelings keep betraying us.

Hey, I've been there myself—multiple times. Every girl I dated for any notable period of time was because I felt like

I loved her, and I thought we were therefore going to be together forever. But, of course, we're not. I've long since split up with every girl I ever thought I was "in love with" except for Monica. And even when dating Monica, I still had those crazy highs and lows: "I love you!" "I hate you!" "Uh, I love you again!" The reason we're still together, and have been relatively happily married all these years, has very little to do with fluctuating feelings. It's because we've redefined what real love looks like.

Love Is a Verb

It's true that love is a feeling. That is one definition of the word. It's a noun, because a feeling is a thing. It's a thing you experience; it's something that happens to you.

However, there's another definition of *love* listed right alongside it in the dictionary. And that's love as a verb. It's an action. It's something you do, not something that happens to you. You can actively care for someone, cherish them as valuable, and look after their best interests.

That's a hugely important difference, because an action is something you control. You can't always choose how you feel (although, through your actions, you can heavily influence your feelings). But you can always choose how you act.

You can't guarantee you will feel a certain way about someone every day for the rest of your life. In fact, it would be fairer to say it's guaranteed you *won't* feel the exact same way about them. There are times I still get butterflies in my stomach when I see Monica, and days when I still feel the same excitement I did when we were first dating or first married. But there are many other times when I don't have those same feelings. Honestly, sometimes I don't have strong feelings for her at all. But that's OK. That's not a crisis in our marriage. Because even if I don't *feel* in love with her, I can still *actively* love her in the things I say and do. I can serve her selflessly, speak to her kindly, and pursue her faithfully. Those things are choices that are always fully in my control. And that's why I can know I will always love Monica, regardless of how I feel, until death do us part.

Interestingly, when you actively love someone in this way, your feelings will follow. If I behave lovingly toward my wife, I can't help but feel love for her as well. It's part of how God has wired us as humans. Your brain wants your words and actions to match up with your feelings. So, for example, if you act like you're excited about something (even when you're not), one of two things will have to happen. Either you'll start to feel excited, or you'll stop acting excited. And since you can choose your actions, you can decide what your feelings will be.

Selfless Love

I officiate weddings every now and then. Before the wedding day, when I first meet with the bride- and groom-to-be, I always ask them, "Why do you love him/her?" One of the more common answers I get is, "Well, I love the way he makes me feel," or "I love how she makes me feel."

I call them out on that. "Man, that sounds incredibly selfish. What you love about him is about you? You don't love her for who she is but just for how she makes you feel? What happens when they can't make you feel exactly the same way anymore? If your main goal is chasing a feeling, I'm concerned for your relationship—because, eventually, the easiest way to get that feeling will be to start chasing after someone else."

If your relationship is based on what they can do *for* you (or what you can do *to* them), that's selfish. It's self-love. You don't even love them; you just love yourself.

Real love is selfless. It's about serving, not being served; giving, not getting. And when both people love and give and serve each other selflessly, well, you end up getting quite a lot.

Feelings Fail; Love Doesn't

We have a model for this kind of love, and this model is Jesus. When we say "God is love" (1 John 4:8), we're not saying God is a feeling; we're saying he defines and exemplifies what love is. And the ultimate expression of that was God sending his Son to sacrifice his life on our behalf, not because we'd done anything good to earn that love but rather because we have all sinned and done wrong.[b] God's love for us isn't just a feeling; it's the most selfless act of service imaginable.[c]

God invented love, so he gets to define it—not Hollywood, television, or the songs you're listening to. God defines it. And the Bible gives God's definition of love in 1 Corinthians 13, known to many as "the love chapter." You've probably heard this passage recited at weddings:

> Love is patient, love is kind. It does not envy, it does not boast, it is not proud. It does not dishonor others, it is not

b. 1 John 4:10: "This is love: not that we loved God, but that he loved us and sent his Son as an atoning sacrifice for our sins."

c. Romans 5:7–8: "Very rarely will anyone die for a righteous person, though for a good person someone might possibly dare to die. But God demonstrates his own love for us in this: While we were still sinners, Christ died for us."

self-seeking, it is not easily angered, it keeps no record of wrongs. Love does not delight in evil but rejoices with the truth. It always protects, always trusts, always hopes, always perseveres. Love never fails. (1 Cor. 13:4–8)

What does that describe? Not a feeling. All of those are things you do, not things you feel. That's why "love never fails." Feelings would sometimes fail, but since love is an action, you can always love someone regardless of how you might feel at the moment.

This list is also all acts of selfless service. If you want to love someone, these are your instructions. This is your job description. Be patient, kind, humble ("does not boast . . . [is] not proud"), respectful ("does not dishonor others"), selfless ("not self-seeking"), gentle ("not easily angered"), forgiving ("keeps no record of wrongs"), forgiven ("does not delight in evil"), truthful, protecting, trusting, hopeful, persevering, and faithful ("never fails"). That's how you are to love. And when you are searching for someone to marry, look for someone who also does these things.

Stop Being Childish

If you are accustomed to chasing feelings, this will likely require a bit of retraining. First Corinthians 13:11 says, "When I was a child, I talked like a child, I thought like a child, I reasoned like a child. When I became a man, I put the ways of childhood behind me."

It's time to put childish, immature ways of dating behind you. My daughter may have been terrible with cats when she was three, but she's gotten over that. She's still a kid, but she's no longer little. She's learned how to love cats without causing pain in the process.

If you're closer to age thirty than age three, it's time for you to do the same in your dating life. Stop hurting people (and stop getting hurt yourself). Stop letting fleeting feelings determine your fate.

Don't Follow Your Heart

The world says to "follow your heart" in dating and in life. That's terrible advice. Your "heart" just means your feelings, and your feelings have no wisdom or insight of their own. Your feelings don't know what is best for you, and they don't care. And since your feelings are always changing, following your heart means you're going to be constantly changing direction.

Woody Allen famously said, "The heart wants what it wants. There's no logic to those things. You meet someone and you fall in love and that's that."[1] Of course, he said that quote in reference to starting a sexual relationship with someone who was essentially his stepdaughter.[d] The heart wants what it wants—but that doesn't mean it should get what it wants.

In stark contrast to "follow your heart," the Bible says, "The heart is deceitful above all things and beyond cure. Who can understand it?" (Jer. 17:9). Your heart is not just

---

d. Soon Yi is the daughter of Mia Farrow, Woody Allen's long-term girlfriend. Because Woody and Mia never officially married, Soon Yi is not legally his stepdaughter. However, she is the half sister of his own children, and is now stepmother to her own siblings.

unreliable; it's *deceitful*. It lies. It will actively lead you astray, if you let it.

Your heart is especially deceitful if you've trained it to be that way—if you've fed it with all the lies that society and the media say about love, and then put those lies into practice. If you look in the rearview mirror and see a string of broken dating relationships and broken hearts, the culprit will also be in the mirror staring back at you. The common denominator in every failed relationship you've ever had is *you*. You've been following your heart to the wrong kind of person, because your heart is programmed incorrectly.

Your heart wants what it wants. You need to train it to want something else. Don't lose hope; this is possible, and it might be easier than you think.

Retrain Your Heart

The Bible never says you should follow your heart. Instead, it says you should guard it. Proverbs 4:23 says, "Above all else, guard your heart, for everything you do flows from it." *Above all else*, guard your heart. In a book of wisdom written by the wisest man to ever live, it says that your heart should be guarded more than anything. Guard it more than gold, money, or your baseball card collection. Why? Because everything you do flows from it. What you set your heart on is what you seek after. It sets the direction for your life. It's your GPS. And in order for your GPS to get you where you want to go, you have to enter in the right destination.

How do you guard your heart? By being careful what you feed it. Your heart tends to want what you see, what you hear, and what you think about all day long.

This means that what you consume—TV shows, movies, music, books, video games, Instagram accounts, Pinterest boards, whatever—actually does have a huge impact on your life. Before you roll your eyes at the cliché of having a pastor warn you about the dangers of your favorite TV show, I can prove it to you with just one word: *advertising*. If what you watch didn't have a huge influence on what you do in real life, then the entire advertising industry wouldn't exist. Think about it. When a company spends millions of dollars to air an ad during the Super Bowl, they don't list facts or features of their product to convince you to buy. Instead, they show images of happy people and trust that you'll want what those people have (and buy their product to get it). Or they try to be funny and entertain you, knowing that entertainment will translate into action and cause people to change their shopping habits. It's true; our whole consumer economy is built on this fact. What you feed your senses fuels your heart.

In a way, your heart works like Netflix.[e] Here's what I mean by that. When I log on to Netflix, it starts giving me suggestions for what it thinks I would like to watch. How does it know what I would like to watch? It sees what I've already watched and the shows I tend to binge, and it makes predictions based on that information. It also has data on millions of different users, so it can calculate the correlations: people who watch *this* show almost always end up watching *this other* show also. "Oh, you like action movies and rom-coms? I bet you'll like *these* movies. You watched a British comedy? We've got tons more like that. You spent last weekend watching *Dora the Explorer* and *My Little Pony*?

e. Or Amazon, YouTube, Disney+, or just about any online service these days.

Then . . . hopefully you have kids. But, anyway, here's some more kids' shows you might like."

Your heart does the same thing. Whatever you watch, whatever you binge, whatever you focus your eyes and your mind on, your heart will start seeking more of the same. If you watch unrealistic "reality" dating shows, then your heart will seek unrealistic relationships. If you sing along with music that objectifies women, you will tend to objectify women. Or if you listen to songs that make it OK to be used, you might look to be used. If you watch pornography once, that doesn't mean you'll be satisfied and not want to watch it again; you'll become *more* likely to seek it out again and to want to act it out in real life. And when you pin yet another dress to that wedding day Pinterest board, you focus your heart on the fairy tale of a one-day party rather than preparing for the reality of the thousands of days that will come after that (or, possibly, before).

Of course, it's not just the media you consume that can send your heart searching. It's the places you choose to go, the friends you choose to hang out with, the celebrities you choose to idolize, and the people you choose to date (or pine over and wish you could date). Whatever you feed your heart, that's what it will chase after.

You reprogram your heart by changing what you feed it. You turn your time and attention away from the lies of popular culture, pornography, social media, or whatever it is you find most seductive, and you turn it toward activities like studying the Bible, learning useful skills, developing new habits, or deploying your gifts to serve others through volunteer work. You may need to "change your playmates and your playground,"[2] as people often say in addiction recovery, choosing to no longer associate with people or places that lead you astray.

What your heart seeks after won't change immediately; it's a process that will take time. The last time I moved, the GPS app on my phone kept trying to send me to all the old places I used to visit. It was used to me typing in certain locations, and it was trained to assume I wanted to go to those places. But, eventually, it learned I wasn't going there anymore. I had new places I wanted to go, closer to my new home. It stopped trying to direct me to my old neighborhood and started auto-correcting to my new destinations. The same thing happens to your heart when you consistently tell it to seek after a 1 Corinthians 13 kind of love instead of the emotional train wrecks it is used to.

Don't follow your heart; inform your heart. Teach it where you want to go.

Healthy Boundaries

There's another aspect of guarding your heart that probably gets more attention, and is what people tend to think of first when they hear the phrase. This is the idea of not "falling in love" with someone too quickly and thereby protecting yourself from heartbreak. There is a lot of truth to that, although it can be misconstrued sometimes.

The goal is not to be an unfeeling robot. Yes, we want to introduce a healthy dose of logic to the process of dating, and we don't want to be driven by emotions. But that doesn't mean we won't have feelings, or that our God-given emotions are inherently bad.

The point is that you shouldn't feed the feelings. Your goal in dating someone is . . . wait, do you know what your goal in dating is by now? It's not to "fall in love" with them, or to convince them to fall in love with you. It's to determine whether they would make a good spouse for you, and whether you can each commit to each other and trust that the other person is equally committed. I would certainly expect feelings to accompany that decision; they just shouldn't be the basis for it.

The Bible says we shouldn't awaken love before its time.[f] Its time would be in marriage, when you have the kind of lifelong commitment that can justify and support any feelings of love, no matter how intense.

How do you keep from awakening love before its time? You set boundaries. Guys, this would be a good chance to show your leadership and provide clarity in dating. You set physical boundaries, since premature feelings are commonly caused by premature intimacy. You set emotional boundaries by agreeing not to tell each other "I love you" until you can be sure you really mean it—and have already proven it, without words, in how you serve each other. And you set spiritual boundaries by not getting into deep, intense prayer sessions together—which is one of the most intimate and vulnerable things you can do with another person.

Also, it is worth pointing out: if you're not even dating someone at all, you definitely shouldn't be giving your heart away to them. I've seen that happen way too many times.

f. Song of Songs 8:4: "Daughters of Jerusalem, I charge you: Do not arouse or awaken love until it so desires." Song of Songs 2:7 and 3:5 say almost exactly the same thing, but with some wildlife thrown in.

Somebody comes crying to me because the person they "love"—someone they've never dated and perhaps have never even officially met—has started dating someone else. That's not how love is supposed to work. That is kind of the opposite of guarding your heart.

Guarding Other People's Hearts

Since real love is about service and seeking the other person's welfare first, it's good practice to also guard other people's hearts.

What does that look like? It means not leading people on, not playing with their emotions because it strokes your ego. It means setting appropriate boundaries when you are dating someone; doing so guards not only your heart but theirs too. It also means avoiding "friendationships," where you enjoy getting affirmation from people of the opposite sex, but you're not actually interested in them and you assume they understand you're just friends. Don't assume, and don't play around with others' hearts. (I just heard someone say "Amen!")

What If Heartache Was Never Part of God's Plan for Us?

Because most people don't marry the first person they date, it's likely that you will face breakups in your life. However, breaking up doesn't have to equal breaking your heart.

Here's a thought: What if heartache was never part of God's plan for us? What if he never intended for us to experience what it's like to have a broken heart? I honestly believe that is the case. He has no desire to see you hurting. I believe it was God's design that you would give your heart away exactly one time, to the person you marry and spend the rest of your life with. That is God's ideal. Of course, since sin and death entered the world, we rarely get to experience the ideal. But we can at least strive toward it, and avoid the world's tendency to give our hearts away to every cute person we meet.

In our fallen world, experiencing some disappointment or hurt is probably unavoidable. But most of our modern heartbreak stems from how we date. It is, to an extent, avoidable. And it is my heart for you that you would avoid that hurt.

6

A Perfect Match

THE LIE: you have to find someone who likes all the same things you do.

THE TRUTH: you just need to find someone with one major common interest.

I have a somewhat unusual hobby: I like to buy and sell things. I'll buy an item from someone, then turn around and sell it to someone else, hopefully at a profit. It's something I've always done in my spare time. Some people play fantasy football, some people plant gardens, some people knit. Me, I buy and sell stuff on Craigslist. It's my side hustle, in addition to being a pastor. I'm the Craigslist pastor.

Here's an example: I had this golf cart I'd bought. I don't play golf; I was just able to get a good deal on it and figured I could sell it for more than what I'd paid. I listed it for sale on Craigslist. A guy sent me a message that said, "Hey, I'll trade you my Toyota Corolla for it." A car for a golf cart? Sure, I said. I'll make that trade. Now I was the not-so-proud owner of a used Toyota Corolla. That wasn't very exciting, so I turned around and sold the Corolla, managing to get more for it than the golf cart had been worth.

Now I had this cash from selling the Corolla, and I started looking for something else to buy with that cash. You know, to keep the chain going. Keep increasing the value. I was looking at my options online, and I saw something called a Polaris Slingshot for sale. A Slingshot is sort of a cross between a car and a motorcycle. It has two car-style seats, and you drive it like a car. But it only has three wheels—one in back, two in front—and it doesn't have any doors or even a roof. In other words, it's super-impractical, but it looks super cool—basically, the opposite of a Toyota Corolla. I took one look at the pictures of this thing, with its sports-car-red paint and racing stripes, and thought, *I've got to have that.*

I didn't think I could afford it, but I talked to the guy who was selling it, and he gave me what seemed like a crazy-good deal on it. And since my heart was already set on having it, I jumped at the offer. I thought, *Hey, I have to lock up this deal before he sells it to someone else.*

So I bought the Slingshot. I started with a golf cart, and now I had this cool sports-car-tricycle thing. Not bad, right? But then, the very first day I had it, the check engine light came on. Soon after that, another light came on; this one said "brake failure." Yeah. That's not a great thing to see while driving your hot-rod tricycle with no roof and no doors.

I knew I couldn't drive it like that, so I started calling around to find a place that could fix it. It wasn't easy; the first seven dealerships I called said they don't work on Slingshots. But the eighth place knew what I was talking about; they were experts in that type of vehicle. I asked the guy on the phone how much it would likely cost to repair it, based on the error messages. He told me, "Well, it depends, but it could be ten thousand."

"Ten thousand dollars?!" I replied, shocked. "Are you serious? That's more than I paid for it."

Then he said, "You should have brought it in before buying it. We could have inspected it. We have these six-point checkups that identify stuff like that. We could have told you there were problems before you decided to buy it."

"Thanks, buddy."

He was right, of course. That's exactly what I should have done. I was too focused on how cool it looked and the seemingly great deal I was getting. But I was looking at all the wrong things. I should have been checking under the hood.

This is what we do in dating. We don't know what to look for, or we simply look at all the wrong things. And once we figure out we were looking at the wrong things, it is sometimes too late. We've already bought. We're committed. And now the cost to fix what's wrong may be more than we are willing to pay.

The Compatibility Myth

Who should you date? That is the question. Out of all the people in the world, who are you supposed to pursue? How do you decide?

When considering who you should date, one thing people talk a lot about is the idea of compatibility. As in, you just have to find someone you're compatible with. If you can find someone you're compatible with, it will work out. You won't have disagreements or differences or conflict or compromises. Why? Because you're compatible. You're of the same type. You're naturally wired to get along.

However, that concept of compatibility is pure fiction. There is no compatibility among sinners—and we are all sinners. We are all flawed. We're all selfish. And if you take a female sinner and a male sinner and you put them together, there are going to be differences. And conflict. Maybe not on day one (or date one), but if we're talking about spending a lifetime together in marriage, there will be plenty of times when you don't get along. There will have to be compromise. So dating is not about finding someone you're compatible with. It's about finding someone you can live with in an understanding way.

Today, with apps, websites, and compatibility tests, we have more ways to help us find a compatible partner than ever before. However, marriages are not more successful as a result, because compatibility is a myth.

The List

In an attempt to define exactly who they are "compatible" with, a lot of people put together a checklist of what they are looking for in a significant other/spouse. In a way, that seems like a great idea. I'm not opposed to having a list, if it's the right kind of list.

The problem is that people almost always put the wrong things on the list. They want a girl who is short or a guy who is tall. They look for a certain hair color or a certain skin color. Their list includes things such as wanting someone who enjoys sports, watches the same obscure TV shows, or likes to eat sushi. There may be quantifiable numbers involved, like someone who makes at least a certain amount of money or who is no older than a certain age.

If your list looks like that, then you are focusing on the wrong attributes. None of those things really matter—or at least they shouldn't. If money is on your list, then you're not interested in them; you're interested in their money. If physical attributes are on your list, then you're not interested in them; you're interested in their body—the one thing about them that is guaranteed to change over time.

Even interests change. I understand wanting to like the same things, because it gives you fun things you can do together. It seems to make sense. But people change. If the basis of your relationship is that you both have the same taste in movies, foods, or vacation destinations, what happens when your tastes change?

I've seen this happen in marriages time and time again. When Monica and I first got married, we loved going on cruises together. We enjoyed all of the activities on a cruise ship: the concerts, the food, hitting golf balls off the back of the ship, shuffleboard—you name it. We went all-in on the cruise experience. It was kind of our thing. It was one of our answers to the question, "So, what do you guys enjoy doing?" "We love to go on cruises." But then, several years into marriage, things changed. Monica said she no longer wanted to go on cruises. It just wasn't nearly as fun for her anymore. So I left her at home. Just kidding. We stopped going on cruises. We found other ways to spend our vacation time together.

If my love for my wife was conditional on her love of cruises, we'd be in trouble. But since that was never the basis for our relationship, it's OK. We can change together.

Letting the Algorithm Decide

Since this is the Age of Apps, people tend to take their checklists and go online to search for their perfect match. The idea is, with so many people to choose from, why not let computers do the hard work of sorting through them all and finding the ones who are compatible? People often ask me if it is OK for Christians to use dating apps or websites. One answer I give to that is I'm sad people would have to, or that they would at least feel like they have to. I'm sad that people aren't just meeting offline, preferably at church or through serving together, and getting to know each other in real life. I'm sad that good guys often aren't asking good girls out in person and are hiding behind the wall of technology instead.

Scripture says that, although we have a lot of freedom to do what we want, not everything is beneficial or helpful.[a] I feel like online dating is one of those things that is not always beneficial, and that frankly I wish wasn't necessary. But am I prepared to say it's absolutely wrong? No. There's nothing in the Bible that says we can't use dating apps. It's not a sin. There are sinful ways we can use dating apps, but it's not a sin in and of itself. And I do know people in God-honoring marriages who met online. I celebrate that fact and have even officiated some of their weddings.

When it comes to dating apps or websites, I would say to be wise and be cautious. There are some principles you should follow if you venture into that world.

a. 1 Corinthians 10:23: "'I have the right to do anything,' you say—but not everything is beneficial. 'I have the right to do anything'—but not everything is constructive."

First, it's obvious that not all apps are created equal. I'm not here to recommend certain ones; as a faithfully married man, I'm not using any dating apps, let alone testing out all the different options. But it's clear that different apps have different priorities. And if the main way people use the app is to look at profile pictures and swipe left or right based solely on whether they think the person is attractive, that's a terrible way to get a match. That's saying you only care about one thing, and it's completely the wrong thing. There's a reason why apps like that are widely known as "hookup apps."

Second, remember that people can lie in their profiles. People are trying to present the best version of themselves online. It's true for social media, and it's doubly true for dating profiles. For example, if you're going to choose a profile picture, you're not going to pick just any photo of yourself. You're going to pick the *best* photo of yourself, from your best angle, with the perfect background, and usually from at least a couple of years ago. And that's just the photo. At least that (presumably) will be some version of the real person. In all the other fields, where people type in their "about me" and all those details and interests you will compare against your checklist, they can write whatever they think you want to hear. I don't care if his profile says he graduated from seminary, he loves Jesus with all his heart, and he cares for the widows and orphans. He could be a con man, optimizing his keywords for a particular target market. Even if that's not the case, and even if everyone online were trying to be more or less honest, you know they're going to be honest about the good parts of themselves and just neglect to mention the bad parts. So always take that into consideration.

Third, be careful. It's possible that cute college coed you've been chatting with is actually a fifty-year-old guy who lives in his mom's basement and loves to fish. I'm not trying to be a fearmonger here; I realize that is highly unlikely. But it is possible. There is nothing preventing it from happening, and there are a number of confirmed cases where it has happened, #catfished.

Finally, if you are going to use online dating, don't do it in isolation. Up until just a few years ago, and for many decades before that, most couples met through friends or family. But now that online dating has taken off, the number of people meeting through friends or family has dropped sharply.[1] What that means is you no longer have people who care about you and who are invested in your well-being helping you make dating decisions. Online dating makes it easier to date in isolation, choosing what you want without the perspective or advice of unbiased, trustworthy friends. In fact, that's one theory for why online dating has become so popular: people don't want to listen to advice from others.[2] But ignoring the advice of people who love you, who want what is best for you and have no ulterior motives in that regard, and especially who can counsel you with God's wisdom from Scripture, is a very unwise thing to do. It's foolish.[b] It means you're ignoring one of your greatest resources in dating. So, if your Christ-following friends and family can't help you find a good match offline, at least bring them into the process of trying to find one online.

b. Proverbs 12:15: "The way of fools seems right to them, but the wise listen to advice."

The Incompatibility Myth

Whereas most people think you should find someone you are *compatible* with, there's another subset focused on finding someone *incompatible*.

I'm talking about the old cliché "Opposites attract." It often takes the form of another popular saying, "Good girls like bad boys," although occasionally that can become reversed. It seems like the problems with that should be obvious, but obviously for many people they are not. I find this theory confusing. Why should a "good" girl like a "bad" guy? Why pursue a relationship with someone who will treat you badly? You can't be surprised when a "bad boy" treats you badly; it's literally part of his description! Why would you sign up for that? It just doesn't make sense, and it's led to a lot of pain due to a lot of ill-advised relationships.

I think there is a self-worth problem at play here; some people don't think they deserve better, so they settle for someone who treats them poorly. Just a quick but important reminder: God took great joy in designing you.[c] He loves you, has given you infinite value, and has paid a great price for you through his Son, Jesus. Find someone with that faith who understands your worth.

I'm not denying that opposites can, in fact, "attract." We are naturally attracted to people who are "other" than us, or who are different in some way. Men and women are typically very different creatures, and those differences are part of the attraction. And, to the extent that those differences complement each other, they can be a good thing. A

c. See Psalm 139, especially verses 13–16.

talker and a listener can make sense together, for example, or someone who is good at planning can balance out a more spontaneous spouse.

But "complement" and "conflict" are two very different things. If you are talking about someone who is your opposite in their values, worldview, or core beliefs, then that kind of attraction is just luring you into a trap. You're getting yourself into a relationship that has nowhere to go. You are opposites; your natural state is to clash. It might seem exciting at first, like you are entering a whole new world. But there are only three ways that story can end.

One, you can break up. Often it's a very dramatic breakup, because of the clash in values. Two, you stay together, but you are constantly in conflict. Not minor conflicts, like disagreeing about where to go for dinner; those happen in any relationship. I'm talking about major conflicts, like 24/7 knock-down, drag-out fights over differences in core beliefs and life goals.

The third option is that, in order to avoid or resolve those conflicts, one of you will have to change. Change can be a good thing, and in healthy relationships (including nonromantic friendships) you can grow and sharpen each other.[d] But when you have fundamental differences, you have to change in a fundamental way. You have to become a different person. And if you like who you are now, then you won't like who you become. If you are more or less on the right track now, striving to follow God and grow in Christlikeness, then changing to accommodate your opposite will only derail you.

d. Proverbs 27:17: "As iron sharpens iron, so one person sharpens another."

Different Directions

The biggest way in which two people can be opposites is in their beliefs about God. That's eternally opposite. That's a difference in how you view the universe, life, your purpose—everything.

Or it should be. I'm regularly approached by people who call themselves Christians but are dating (or considering dating, or even considering marrying) people who are not. Often they are seeking approval for the relationship. Is it OK? Can a Christian date a non-Christian?

Can they? Let me change the question slightly. Can someone who is fully devoted to following Christ date someone who is not a Christian? The answer to that is a definitive no. Not "No, they *shouldn't*," but "No, they *can't*." They literally can't. Because if you choose to date someone who is not a Christian, then you yourself are not following God's instructions. You might be saved, but you're sinning by going against God's life-giving instruction for you. So instead of having someone fully following Christ dating someone who is not, you just have two people who are both not following Christ dating each other.

Second Corinthians 6:14 is the most famous verse that addresses this question. It's the "Do not be yoked together with unbelievers" verse.[e] It's a super-practical command; as the rest of the verse and the verses following it spell out, the problem is that a believer and a nonbeliever have nothing in

e. Although 2 Corinthians 6:14 does not explicitly say the word *marriage*, marriage is still the clearest example of how two people could be "yoked together." In other words, although it might apply to any kind of close relationship, it definitely includes marriage in that category. Other verses, including 1 Corinthians 7:39, do explicitly say that believers should not marry unbelievers.

common—or at least nothing important.[f] Sure, you might like the same kind of music, or enjoy a few of the same activities. But the very basis of your life—the reason behind every decision, every goal, every life choice—is different. You have completely different missions and different ideas of where you came from and where you are going. The most important thing in your life is, in their mind, either a myth or a lie. To them, you're either deceived or crazy. To you, they are lost and destined for an eternity apart from you. You can never truly connect and achieve oneness in marriage with that kind of foundation.

But the concept of being equally "yoked" goes beyond just having the same general beliefs. The metaphor would have been obvious to the Corinthians, because in those days yokes were common. People used them all the time; they were employed to hitch two oxen or other animals together so they could pull a wagon or plow. Myself, I'd never even seen a yoke until a couple of years ago, when I came upon one in a museum. Let me describe it to you. A yoke is a big wooden beam—think several times thicker and stronger than a two-by-four; a piece of wood you could never even think about bending or breaking—that is fitted to sit across the shoulders of two oxen, on the backs of their necks. There are then two wooden U-shaped pieces that go around the front of the animals' necks and lock into place at each end of the beam. Once fastened to each other in this way, the two animals are "yoked together."

f. 2 Corinthians 6:14–16: "Do not be yoked together with unbelievers. For what do righteousness and wickedness have in common? Or what fellowship can light have with darkness? What harmony is there between Christ and Belial? Or what does a believer have in common with an unbeliever? What agreement is there between the temple of God and idols? For we are the temple of the living God."

The result of being "yoked together," therefore, is that the two of you have to be going exactly the same direction, at exactly the same speed, at all times. There is no other option; you're connected at the neck with an unbreakable, unbendable wooden beam. If one of you turns left, the other has to turn left too; if not, you'll end up breaking your necks. If one of you stops, the other one has to do the same, or else you'll be pulled off to the side and will wind up in the ditch.

When you are looking for someone to be "yoked together" with, it is essential to find someone who is going the same direction in life, and at the same speed. You want someone who is running after Christ as you are, with the same level of devotion. Because they are either going to be helping you carry your load or actively dragging you down. They're either going your direction or pulling you somewhere you don't want to go.

What You Should Look For

What you are looking for, therefore, is someone who is a fully devoted follower of Christ. First you have to be one yourself, then you find someone else who is similarly pursuing God and join together in your pursuit.

How can you tell if someone is following Christ? You can't just ask them, because they might lie, or they might answer honestly but have a completely different definition of what it means. And you also can't assume they are because you saw them at church; going to church doesn't make you a Christian any more than going to McDonald's makes you a hamburger.

Here's where a different kind of checklist can come in handy. When I bought the Slingshot sports-car-tricycle thing, I should have first gone to the experts and let them inspect it. They would have gone through their checklist of the important things to look for—things that are not superficial or obvious at first sight but which are essential for determining how well it will run and whether it will be likely to break down in the future.

When it comes to relationships, or human beings in general, God is the expert. He created people, and he created marriage. So if you want to know what to look for in a potential spouse, you go to him and his Word. The Bible has some great descriptions of what an ideal husband or wife looks like, in places like Proverbs 31 or 1 Timothy 3. By studying the Bible, you can create a list of what you should really be looking for—the things that mark the life of someone who is following God.

If you take those traits from the Bible, they will play out in a person's life in ways you can see and observe. You should be looking for someone who is:

- **Controlled.** We all sin at times, but you want someone who can control the parts of themselves that need to be controlled. You want to look for someone who is gentle,[g] patient,[h] peaceful,[i] and modest;[j]

---

g. 1 Timothy 3:2–3: "Now the overseer is to be above reproach, faithful to his wife, temperate, self-controlled, respectable, hospitable, able to teach, not given to drunkenness, not violent but gentle, not quarrelsome, not a lover of money."

h. Ephesians 4:2: "Be completely humble and gentle; be patient, bearing with one another in love."

i. Romans 12:18: "If it is possible, as far as it depends on you, live at peace with everyone."

j. 1 Peter 3:3–4: "Your beauty should not come from outward adornment, such as elaborate hairstyles and the wearing of gold jewelry or fine clothes. Rather, it should someone who can say no to worldly passions that would end up hurting them or hurting you.[k] If someone's life is currently marked by repeated, ongoing, unrepentant sin, then they fail this particular test. As you observe how they live, ask yourself, are they marked by self-control?

* **Responsible.** Seek out someone who is diligent,[l] taking care of what needs to be done, when it needs to be done. You want someone who is willing to work hard, because marriage takes work. You also want them to be responsible in how they work to earn and steward resources, so that they can provide for your family.[m] This does *not* mean that they need to make a lot of money, because the goal is not to be rich on this earth.[n] But someone who works hard and diligently will always be able to provide enough; I've seen it firsthand in even the poorest of countries. And before you think I'm talking primarily about men here, being a hard worker applies equally to both sexes in the Bible. Much of Proverbs 31, which is about "the wife of

be that of your inner self, the unfading beauty of a gentle and quiet spirit, which is of great worth in God's sight."

k. Titus 2:12: "It teaches us to say 'No' to ungodliness and worldly passions, and to live self-controlled, upright and godly lives in this present age."

l. Proverbs 21:5: "The plans of the diligent lead to profit as surely as haste leads to poverty."

m. 1 Timothy 5:8: "Anyone who does not provide for their relatives, and especially for their own household, has denied the faith and is worse than an unbeliever."

n. Matthew 6:19–21: "Do not store up for yourselves treasures on earth, where moths and vermin destroy, and where thieves break in and steal. But store up for yourselves treasures in heaven, where moths and vermin do not destroy, and where thieves do not break in and steal. For where your treasure is, there your heart will be also."

noble character," is spent talking about all the ways in which she works diligently. Ask yourself, would you trust this person to be responsible for your future children?

- **Obedient.** Look for someone who listens to and obeys wise counsel, who is humble enough to be teachable[o] and wise enough to realize there is a lot they don't know.[p] They should be someone who doesn't just obey their own desires but who instead willingly submits to and obeys both Christ and his church. Part of God's provision for us is that we can seek advice and learn from other believers, which is why we are commanded to be part of a local community of believers[q] and to submit to church elders.[r] If someone is actively choosing to not be part of a local body of believers, then they are not part of the body of Christ,[s] and you shouldn't consider joining yourself to them. Ask yourself, are they living as their own king or queen, or are they obedient to the true King?

o. Psalm 25:9: "He guides the humble in what is right and teaches them his way."

p. Proverbs 12:15: "The way of fools seems right to them, but the wise listen to advice."

q. Hebrews 10:24–25: "And let us consider how we may spur one another on toward love and good deeds, not giving up meeting together, as some are in the habit of doing, but encouraging one another—and all the more as you see the Day approaching." And many other verses.

r. Hebrews 13:17: "Have confidence in your leaders and submit to their authority, because they keep watch over you as those who must give an account. Do this so that their work will be a joy, not a burden, for that would be of no benefit to you." 1 Peter 5:5: "In the same way, you who are younger, submit yourselves to your elders. All of you, clothe yourselves with humility toward one another, because, 'God opposes the proud but shows favor to the humble.'"

s. See 1 Corinthians 12:12–31.

- **Serving.** You want a spouse who is selfless,[t] kind,[u] and compassionate.[v] You want them to be that way toward *you*, and the best evidence for that is how they already treat others in their lives, and especially how they treat people who can't really do anything for them in return. This means they'll be serving somewhere. Maybe it's volunteering in the kids' ministry at church, stopping to help people who have flat tires on their cars, or using their vacation time to serve "the least of these"[w] in an underprivileged country. Note that a true servant won't make a big deal out of their service; you won't hear them proudly broadcasting the fact they are out there looking after the widows and orphans.[x] But when you go where the servants are, they will be there. Ask yourself, would they be described as having a servant's heart?

- **Steady.** Obviously, you want to marry someone you can trust,[y] someone who is faithful,[z] honest,[aa] and lives out what they say they believe. What this means

t. Ephesians 5:25: "Husbands, love your wives, just as Christ loved the church and gave himself up for her."

u. 2 Timothy 2:24: "And the Lord's servant must not be quarrelsome but must be kind to everyone, able to teach, not resentful."

v. Proverbs 31:20: "She opens her arms to the poor and extends her hands to the needy."

w. Matthew 25:40: "The King will reply, 'Truly I tell you, whatever you did for one of the least of these brothers and sisters of mine, you did for me.'"

x. James 1:27: "Religion that God our Father accepts as pure and faultless is this: to look after orphans and widows in their distress and to keep oneself from being polluted by the world."

y. Luke 16:10: "Whoever can be trusted with very little can also be trusted with much, and whoever is dishonest with very little will also be dishonest with much."

z. Proverbs 20:6: "Many claim to have unfailing love, but a faithful person who can find?"

aa. Proverbs 12:22: "The LORD detests lying lips, but he delights in people who are trustworthy."

is you need to look for someone with a reputation—a good reputation. You want someone who has a history of living out the traits on this list. Now, this doesn't mean they don't have a past; we all have a past, and I would encourage you not to rule someone out because of how they behaved in their B.C. (before Christ) days. If that was a disqualifier, I'd be disqualified. They can have a past; you just want to make sure they've moved beyond it and have demonstrated over a sufficiently long period of time they have truly changed. I'm reminded of another time I bought a car under what seemed like questionable circumstances. This car, which I actually planned to drive rather than just resell, had a salvage title. What that means is it had been in a really bad accident, so bad that the insurance company considered it totaled. It was a literal wreck; they didn't think it could be repaired. But then somebody else managed to repair it anyway. Now, a lot of people would rightly be scared to buy a salvaged car, because it could have all sorts of hidden problems. But I looked up its vehicle history report and saw that it had been more than three years since that accident, and it hadn't had a single problem since. It ran perfectly. There were no hidden problems, because a hidden problem would have already reared its head in the three-plus years it had been driven since then. That's what you're looking for: a sufficiently long track period of faithfulness. How long? It depends on what they are recovering from. It might not need to be three years, but it's probably more than six months. Their repentance should be as notorious as their rebellion. Ask your-self, *Do I trust that this person is on a steady trajectory in their life?*

Controlled, Responsible, Obedient, Serving, and Steady. Put those together, and you have someone whose life is marked by the CROSS. (See what I did there? You're welcome. It took a lot of time playing Scrabble to accomplish that.)

Who You Should Be

Those are all things you should look for in a potential spouse. Although there are some variations in what a man should look for in a woman versus what a woman should look for in a man, for the most part you're looking for the same kinds of things, and everything in the list above applies to both sexes.[ab]

And, again, it's not about having a specific list; you're just looking for someone who is fully devoted to following Christ. However, people who are following Christ will naturally do these things and exhibit these traits. They provide evidence you can see for the condition of their heart, which you cannot otherwise see.

Note that since this applies to both women and men, this means I just told everyone out there to look for those things in you, as well. This isn't just a list of what to look for. First and foremost, it's a list of the fruit[ac] that should be occurring in your life. And if that's not the case, you

ab. I did include separate (though similar) lists for men and women in chapter 8 of *Welcome to Adulting*.

ac. Galatians 5:22–23: "But the fruit of the Spirit is love, joy, peace, forbearance, kindness, goodness, faithfulness, gentleness and self-control. Against such things there is no law."

need to examine your heart to identify why it's not. The most loving thing you can do for your future spouse is to get your own life in order long before you even meet them. Not that you have to be perfect—you *won't* be perfect, and neither will they—but you can strive today to grow in Christlikeness.

The Next Step

OK, so we've established the general things you should be looking for, and the fact that what you're really looking for is someone who is a fully devoted follower of Christ. But what now? Out of all the people who potentially meet that description, who specifically should you date?

I can actually tell you that right now. No, I don't know his or her name, so I can't tell you exactly who. But *you* know their name.

It's really simple. We tend to make it so complicated, like we need a whiteboard, a spreadsheet, and a calculus equation to figure it out. It's not like that at all.

Here's what you do. This is probably my single best piece of dating advice, so grab your highlighter. Here it comes.

If you're a man, think of the godliest single woman you know and ask her out on a date. That's it. If you're ready to date, meaning that you desire marriage and getting married in the foreseeable future is a possibility for you, find the godliest unmarried woman you know and ask her out. Not the hottest somewhat-godly woman, or the one who checks the most boxes on your superficial list of physical traits. Not the one you noticed across the room and hope might be godly but you don't really know, because she's still a stranger to you. No, I mean the godliest single woman you know. Full stop. Ask her out. Give her a chance.

And if you're a woman who is similarly ready for marriage, and a godly man approaches you and asks you out on a date, you say yes. You give him a chance. Even if he's not the one you already had your heart set on, or doesn't match up with your "tall, dark, and handsome" fantasies. Now, if he's not godly, or if he's a stranger and you have no way to know whether he is godly or not, you tell him no. You don't waste your time with that. But if he is a godly man—you've observed that he is, or you have trusted friends who know him and can vouch for him—you give him a chance. You're not saying yes to marrying him; we're just talking about one date. After that, you can decide whether you want to continue with a second date.

Is it really that simple? It can be, if you allow it to be. I've seen it happen many times now. You're not trying to find someone "compatible" with you. You want to be someone who is pursuing Christ with your whole life, and then you're trying to find someone else pursuing Christ at the same pace—going the same direction you are at the same speed. And if you're fully yielded to Christ and they're fully yielded to Christ, you don't have to pursue each other. You pursue God together, side by side, as one.

Imagine life as if you're running a race. You're chasing after Jesus. You're serving in your church, going on mission trips, sitting in Bible studies, hanging out with a solid group of friends who are also running after Jesus. As you look to your right or left, there is always someone running alongside you. They are doing the same things you are to chase after Jesus. Find someone running in the same direction you are,

PART 3

how we date

7

Playing Games

THE LIE: you have to be good at playing games to date.

THE TRUTH: you just have to be good at being honest.

There's a famous scene in the movie *Swingers* where two guys are giving dating advice to their friend Mike. Mike has just gotten a woman's phone number at a bar and is wondering when he should call her. Mike's friends advise him to wait before calling, because he doesn't want to seem too interested in her (even though he *is* interested; that's why he got her number). This leads to a discussion on exactly how long he should wait before calling in order to have the desired effect—whether it be one day, two days, three days, or three weeks—with Mike's friends finally saying they prefer to wait six days.

Although it is a fictional comedy and is played for laughs, the advice given by Mike's friends throughout the film is not really any different than the advice given by many real-life friends. (In fact, the reason I use *Swingers* as an example is because I know people who have quoted it to friends as dating advice, turning jokes into serious practice.) And although waiting a specific amount of time to call (or text) might seem fairly benign, it is part of the more invasive idea that you have to play games in dating. It suggests there is a certain psychological calculus you have to know the rules of in order to even have a shot at a successful dating relationship. It would be one thing if that were true; if it were, you could just learn the rules and play the game. However, this is a game where winning is the surest way to guarantee you're actually a loser. The only winning move is not to play.[a]

The Dating Game

What do I mean by "playing games"? What does that look like in dating?

People play games in dating any time they say or do something in order to get a particular response from the other person. We're not talking about fun games but rather mind games. They are little (or big) things people do in order to manipulate others.

There are many ways in which people play games in dating. For example, playing "hard to get" is one super-common, well-known game. (The emphasis is on the "playing" part; you may actually *be* hard to get, but it's only a game if you simply pretend you are.) The idea is that people want what they can't have, so you try to make yourself appear unavailable. Waiting an arbitrarily long period of time before calling

a. Yes, that is a quote from *WarGames*. Bonus points if you got the reference.

or texting someone back is a subset of that, because it shows you're not too eager or interested in the other person. Or maybe you ghost them for a calculated amount of time and take joy in seeing their frantic texts checking in. Then, when they go silent, you reach back out to keep the game alive. That is messed up, and it's not loving.

Some people play games by pretending to be someone they are not. They figure out what the other person is looking for in a mate, and then they falsely act like they are that kind of person. I've sadly seen this in churches, with people who show up and try to give the impression they are Christians, when actually they are predators trying to attract a particular kind of prey. This isn't theoretical; I've had guys admit to doing it. If someone claims to be one thing but their actions soon contradict those claims, believe their actions over their words. People may fail to do what they say, but they rarely fail to do what they believe.

It gets worse. Another "game" some people play is to intentionally undercut the other person's self-esteem, because someone with a lowered self-esteem would then lower their standards to date the loser who is undermining them. This is often closely associated with abusive relationships, because the abused person may come to believe they are not good enough to find someone better, or wrongly feel they somehow deserve to be treated badly.[b]

There are other examples. I won't get into them all here because this is not a guide on how to play games; it's about

---

b. If you are in an abusive dating relationship, get out now. Get safe and get help, if needed. This goes for any kind of abuse, including emotional abuse. You are of infinite worth, and your value is determined by the One who created you, not by what some fallible, sinful person thinks of you—or even by what you think of yourself.

how to avoid them. And all dating games have one thing in common: they are designed to manipulate the other person, using some form of dishonesty or deception. If you're being fully honest with someone, then you are not playing games.

Manipulative Dating

Being honest is far simpler and easier than playing games. You don't have to know any special tactics, tricks, or rules in order to be honest. You don't have to keep track of what lies you've told in order to keep your story consistent, and you don't have to hide anything.

In one obvious example from my own life, as a teen I used a fake ID to get into a club. I met a woman there, and after dancing together most of the night, we started dating. Since I knew she was older than me, and I didn't want to admit to using a fake ID, I lied about my age and embraced that fake identity. I really liked her, but everything was built on this lie I had to keep up. She did eventually learn the truth, and although we kept dating for a while after that, the whole relationship was a nightmare because there was no trust. She (appropriately) did not trust me, so the relationship was doomed from the start. It would have been a lot easier, and more likely to succeed, if I had just been honest from the start.

Since playing games makes dating harder, why do people bother to do it? Why are there books and websites and paid dating coaches people hire in order to learn how to play the game?

It's because, in the short run, manipulation works. That's the whole point of manipulation. If it didn't work, it wouldn't exist; no one would ever go to the trouble of trying to manipulate anyone.

Manipulation works, but it works in all the ways you don't (or shouldn't) want it to. It works to build distrust. It works to create a false relationship that is unsustainable because it is based on lies. Manipulation is about taking advantage of someone, in some form or fashion, for your own short-term gain.

Some "players" use manipulation because the short term is all they care about. They play games because, to them, the games are fun. They enjoy manipulating people. They treat other human beings as playthings, worthy of no more consideration than you would give an inanimate toy. And because the short-term nature of their game gives them plenty of repetition and practice, they get quite good at it. They know how to successfully play with the other person's emotions and get them to compromise their standards in the area of physical intimacy, which often is the whole point of the game. Once they sleep with the other person, they've won and they're done. Time to move on to the next target.

If you are such a person—if you're a player—you need to grow up, and you need to stop. You are out there hurting people, over and over again, and you don't even realize you're hurting yourself in the process. I mean, what do you even call someone who goes around intentionally hurting people? A psychopath?

The Long Game

Others play what you might call a long game. The goal is a long-term relationship with just one person, which is a noble goal, but they believe playing games is the way to get there.

Let's think this through logically. Say you successfully manipulate someone to the point of convincing them to marry you. That happens all the time, by the way. It's entirely possible to marry someone and not know who they truly are; I've heard that story many times. So now what? Are you going to just continue playing games, hiding your true motives, and manipulating each other for the next seventy years? That sounds absolutely exhausting, if it is even possible. And you will never experience the true oneness God designed for marriage, because you're not truly being yourself. Usually, such a marriage ends in divorce, which is one reason the divorce rate is so high.

Some people may object to that, saying that although they do play games, they would never take it that far; that games are for the beginning of a relationship, and once they have the other person "on the hook," they would be honest with them as they move toward marriage. To that I would say: lies are still lies. It's wrong whether you do it for a lifetime, a year, a month, or a minute. And what these folks are literally saying is that, if they were honest, the other person would leave them right at the start, so they have to hook them and trap them before the other person can find out who they really are. That is a fake foundation and a terrible way to look at relationships. Just ask any fish what it's like to be "on the hook." What we really want is someone who will go with us—our real selves—willingly, instead of being strung along.

If you are a game player, here's the truth: you don't realize it, but playing games is what has made you the insecure person you are; you've taught yourself to believe people won't be attracted to your true self.

The goal should be love—real, honest, selfless love. Many dating games are based on the idea of power, and how you can gain or maintain some kind of control over the other person. How is that loving? It is incompatible with love. Love has nothing to do with trying to get the upper hand on someone. Instead, you should be fighting over who gets to be the bigger servant. And you should definitely be looking to date and marry someone who has a servant's heart, not a controlling mind.

Even if you succeed at playing games, you've still lost. You don't want success in dating to be based on how well you've played a game. You want the other person to like you for *you*.

It's easy enough to simply tell you to "stop playing games," but I also have to say it is possible to get so accustomed to playing games that you no longer consciously realize you are doing it. Manipulation becomes your M.O. Therefore, you need to stop and think about *why* you do the things you do in dating. *Am I trying to get a reaction? Am I bending the truth to get them to like me more? Am I behaving differently around this person than I do around my close friends?* Take stock of your motivations and remove any manipulations.

And if you discover that someone is playing games with you, tell them you refuse to play along. If they haven't outgrown playing games, then they are not grown-up enough to make a good husband or wife. It is wrong to date children, no matter how old they might be.

Let's Be Honest

The solution is so simple. Playing games is complicated, which is why people think there are so many rules to dating and the reason they fail is because they don't know all the rules. But when you choose not to play games, there is really only one rule, and it is so simple that anyone can follow it: just be honest.

That's really it. Be honest. Don't lie. Don't pretend to be someone you are not, pretend to be feeling something you are not, or use tricks to try to fool someone. Don't start a relationship based on fraud.

"Simple" doesn't always mean easy. Sometimes telling the truth is hard. For example, suppose you are a woman and a guy asks you out on a date—first date, second date, any date—and you have a good reason to not be interested in him. What do you do? You tell him no, of course. But you have to be honest about it. So it's not "No, I have to rearrange my sock drawer," or "Sorry, I'm committed to not dating anyone right now" (even though you'd say yes in a heartbeat if it was the right guy), or "Sure, let me give you my number," and then you write down the digits to Domino's. Those are lies, and even when you think you're lying for their benefit, lies are never loving. The truly loving thing to do is to tell the truth. The Bible says, "Love must be sincere" (Rom. 12:9) and love "rejoices with the truth" (1 Cor. 13:6); it also says that God hates lies (Prov. 6:16–19; 12:22) and that the devil is "the father of lies" (John 8:44). Even if you're not interested in them in that way, you should still "love your neighbor as yourself" (Matt. 22:39) by letting them know the truth. That may mean telling them you don't see evidence in their life that they are following Christ, and that's a nonnegotiable for you. Or that you've just met and you don't know them well enough to make that judgment, and you are concerned about their motives when they are willing to date you based just on your looks. Or whatever the reason may be. It's loving because it lets them know the reason. Far too often people are blind to their own problems; you don't know if something is "stuck in your teeth," so to speak, unless someone is kind enough to tell you about it. It might be an uncomfortable moment, but being honest gives them the opportunity to improve rather than continually being rejected for a flaw they can't even see.

Being honest can also keep you from being shallow or superficial, because it means you would have to be honest about that too. If you're not interested because you just want someone who is taller, darker, or more handsome, then you admit that and apologize for being shallow. That way, at least they'll know they are not really missing out on anything.

Just tell the truth. The truth is always good enough. The only reason to lie is because you think the truth isn't good enough, and the truth is always good enough. Nowhere in Scripture does it say you should be anything less than honest.

Honest, Not Hurtful

That doesn't mean you have to be hurtful. Remember, ladies, that asking you out is scary. You may not feel intimidating, but you are. As men, it can be terrifying to approach you, look you in the eyes, use our words, and say, "I'd like to go on a date with you." Because there's the unspoken subtext: *Am I worthy? Or will you reject me?*

I've worked in sales, and one of the key things they teach you in sales is how to handle being told no all the time. That's what makes sales hard. It's why most people don't want to do the job. Sales trainers try to overcome that by teaching new salespeople not to take it personally. When you are selling a product and someone tells you they don't want it, they are rejecting the product; they are not rejecting you as a person. But when you ask someone on a date and they tell you no, they *are* rejecting you as a person. You are the thing for sale (metaphorically speaking), and they're not buying. That's hard.

That doesn't mean women should be reluctant to say no or to tell the truth when rejecting someone. Just be conscious that the guy is likely literally afraid of you. If you are intentionally hurtful or mean, you'll just reinforce that fear and make him less likely to ask anyone else out in the future. That may not affect you personally, but some of your girlfriends are out there desperately waiting for someone to have the courage to ask them on a date. Help a sister out. If you're not interested, tell him no and lovingly tell him the truth, so he can correct any blind spots in his own life and be a better man for the next girl he asks on a date.

You can be honest without being hurtful. Conversely, you can ultimately be hurtful by being dishonest in a misguided attempt to protect someone from the truth. As Proverbs 27:6 says, "Wounds from a friend can be trusted, but an enemy multiplies kisses." Here's the test: are you saying it to hurt them or to help them, in the long run, be the person God wants them to be?

And for the men: be a man. Part of being a man is stepping up and facing your fears. I know you feel like she is going to bite your head off and stab you through the heart if you dare ask her on a date, but in reality that rarely happens. (And if it did, it would just serve as confirmation that she's not a good prospect for you.) If you are a godly man who loves Jesus with all your heart, and you desire to find a godly woman to serve selflessly through marriage, then it is worth getting out there and asking. You are outnumbered; there are more godly women who deeply desire to get married than there are godly men who have the guts to ask them out. If you want to serve, I can't think of a bigger service opportunity than that. I know you want to be a hero; this is your chance.

Active, Not Passive

You may have noticed that, so far, I've only talked about men asking out women on dates, and not vice versa. There is a reason for that.

I'm not saying that a woman can't ask a man out on a date. That is allowed. It's not a sin. In the biblical account of Ruth and Boaz, Ruth is the one who takes the first step to initiate the relationship, and the Bible doesn't seem to frown on that.[c]

At the very least, Ruth showed an interest in Boaz, and there is nothing wrong with letting a man know you might be interested in him. In fact, that's just part of being honest; you shouldn't actively pretend you are not interested when you actually are. That would be a lie and a form of the "playing hard to get" game. Letting a man know you are interested can even be an act of service, because, honestly, guys can sometimes be clueless about such things. And that still leaves the ball in his court in terms of deciding whether he wants to ask you out on a date.

But although a woman can ask a man out, I wouldn't necessarily recommend it, for one reason in particular.

c. See Ruth 3. Again, dating didn't exist back then, which is why their cultural method of doing things may seem weird to us today.

You pick your own problems in dating and marriage. Having a passive husband—or, conversely, a controlling wife—is one of the most common root causes of problems in marriage. I've observed that myself, and heard it often from others who are in marriage ministry full-time. By asking a guy out, you might be asking for that problem. At the least, you're choosing someone who has been passive (in terms of not asking you out himself) and enabling him to remain passive.

What does it mean to be passive? A passive man is a passenger in the relationship. Instead of making decisions (such as the decision to get married), he just goes with the flow and takes the path of least resistance. Instead of taking initiative, he just lets things happen. He's not one to willingly work on the relationship or come up with ways to serve you better. Before you think this is outdated thinking, I will just say I have *never* met a woman who didn't want a guy to initiate and clearly communicate his intentions.

Passivity is not a new problem; it's the oldest problem. In the garden of Eden, the very first sin was when Eve and Adam ate the fruit they'd been commanded not to eat. Some (including Adam) have blamed Eve for being the first to take the fruit and then offering it to her husband. However, it was Adam, not Eve, whom God told to leave that fruit alone; Eve hadn't even been created yet (Gen. 2:16–18). It was up to him to teach her the one rule God had given, and he obviously didn't do a very good job. More importantly, when she decided to take the forbidden fruit, Adam was "with her" (3:6); he did nothing to stop her, and he went right along in breaking the one rule when she offered him some to eat. Based on that, you could almost say that male passivity coincided with the original sin.

There are also other examples in the Bible of women who got impatient with waiting on God's timing and decided to take things into their own hands, and the men who passively went along with them. Abraham and Sarah were told that they would have a son (15:4). Instead of trusting God's promise, Sarah thought the only way to have children was to use a surrogate mother instead, and Abraham went along with her plan (16:1–2). That decision had many negative consequences.[d]

This desire to "help" God with his timetable by taking matters into our own hands is often a reflection of us not trusting that God is faithful to keep his promises, and, ladies, that you may not trust a guy to step up and lead you. Don't play that game. If a man's not willing to take initiative, and doesn't see you as being valuable enough to be worth pursuing in dating, then he is not the kind of man you really want to yoke yourself to.

I Wonder . . .

Once you take the initiative to ask someone out on a date (or agree to their ask), you want the relationship to be going somewhere. It should be actively moving toward marriage, and if it's not, it should be quickly moving toward an end to the dating relationship.

That's another lesson I've learned from sales: you don't want to waste time with people who aren't going to buy. A yes is great, but a no is OK too, because it lets you quickly

---

d. See Genesis 21:1–21, and also the modern Israeli-Palestinian conflict. When God did fulfill his promise and gave Sarah a child of her own, she jealously banished the surrogate mother, Hagar, and her son to the desert. Modern Arabs and Palestinians claim Ishmael, the son of Hagar, as their ancestor, while the Israelites are descendants of Sarah's son Isaac. These siblings still haven't found a way to coexist.

move on to someone else. The one answer salespeople can't stand is maybe, because it leaves you in limbo. You don't know whether they're going to buy or not. You have to spend more time with the prospect, and it will likely be a waste of time, because they don't know what they want. You get your hopes up that they might eventually say yes, which makes it even more painful when it (usually) doesn't work out. Either they finally decide the answer is no, or they just never decide anything at all, leaving you forever wondering where they stand and where the relationship is going.

Being honest is the best defense against that kind of confusion. Be clear about your intentions. Remember that people wonder. They wonder what you are thinking. They especially wonder what you think about them. They wonder whether this is a date, or whether there was some other reason you asked them to grab coffee with you. They wonder whether you are interested in a real relationship or are just playing with them and wasting their time. They wonder whether this is going anywhere.

Men, this again falls more squarely on your shoulders. I'm not saying that men don't wonder about these things too; we all know we do. But as much as we wonder about women, know that women typically wonder about us more. Women, on average, are more emotionally complex creatures. Everybody knows that; it's the subject of many a joke in sitcoms and movies.[e] You can serve them well by providing clarity. Let them know what you are thinking, where

e. From *Harry Potter and the Order of the Phoenix*:
Ron Weasley: "One person can't feel all that at once, they'd explode."
Hermione Granger: "Just because you've got the emotional range of a teaspoon doesn't mean we all have."

they stand with you, and how you think things are going. Avoid massive surprises. For example, it's nice for them to be surprised when you propose, but it shouldn't be a shock to them. They should fully know that was your goal, and that the relationship was serious enough and progressing enough that a proposal could come any day. They also shouldn't be shocked if you decide to break up with them. Nothing good comes from making that a surprise. They shouldn't think things are going perfectly in the relationship if you're actually seeing all these red flags.

Women, know that men can't read your mind. On average, men are not as good as women at reading other people's emotions.[1] Don't assume they understand you the way your girlfriends might. You also have to use your words.

Be Clear

How can you be clear and keep the other person from wondering? For starters, make sure it is obvious that you are, in fact, on a date. This shouldn't be that hard, but I have heard of situations where one person thinks it is a date and the other person thinks it is, I don't know, a business meeting or something. Girls, if a guy asks you out, one-on-one, has no business-related agenda, focuses the conversation on learning about you, and pays the bill, that should be evidence it is a date. If he calls soon after to ask you out again, that's a sign he thought it went well.

Guys, if things are going well, ask her out again. Don't wait very long, because then you're just making her wonder: *Will he, or won't he? Are we dating or not?* Don't go on one date in July and then wait until Labor Day to call her up again. And for clarity, just use the word *date*. As in, "Would you like to go on a date with me?"

Leaders remove confusion. Men, you can be better leaders by removing confusion. That may mean you need to explicitly define the relationship. Some people refer to that as a "DTR," where you have a conversation specifically to discuss where you stand with each other. It doesn't need to be a specific event, though; your intentions should be explicitly clear throughout the relationship.

Don't date more than one person at a time. That's confusing. And even if you are clear and honest with both parties, what happens if *both* relationships progress into something serious? It's just an all-around bad idea.

Finally, remember that some forms of communication are clearer than others. Face-to-face conversations are the clearest way to communicate, because so much of what we say is conveyed either nonverbally or through our tone of voice. On the other end of the spectrum, text messaging is probably the worst way to communicate anything of importance, because there is no body language to be seen, no voice to be heard, and not even that many words to give context for what you are saying. You can text about minor things like confirming what time you're meeting up, but it is not a good way to talk through important issues.

Be Intentional

Besides being honest and clear, you need to have a good purpose for dating someone. It's possible to honestly date someone with no plan and no purpose (or at least no good, God-honoring purpose). You can tell them the truth that you have no desire for marriage and that you're only interested in a good time. That would make it an honest game, but you'd still be playing.

You should date intentionally. Dating isn't something that happens by random chance. You don't accidentally end up dating someone, or at least you shouldn't. It should be a conscious decision to go on a date with someone. There should be a purpose and a plan. And that holds true whether it's your first date or your fiftieth date together.

This is different from the trend of "hanging out." Hanging out and having fun with a group of friends is fine, and it can be a good way to get to know someone you may later end up dating. But "hanging out" is now often used to describe relationships that would have once been called "dating." Dating implies at least a little bit of purpose and intentionality, whereas hanging out feels more random. You can "hang out" with anyone: your roommate, your grandma, or a stranger you just met. It doesn't really mean anything, which is exactly why some people use the term to avoid the responsibility of "dating."

The overarching goal of any date should be to determine whether the relationship should move forward—basically, whether there should be another date.[f] For a first date, the goal is to get to know them a little better and to see if you are interested enough to consider a second date. As the relationship progresses and moves closer to marriage, your conversations can get into more detail about your expectations and ideas for how you could build a life

---

f. At least, that's the goal for dates before marriage. You should still date your spouse after marriage, but at that point you're not using the date to decide whether to stay married.

together. It's a good idea not to get that order confused; you don't need to be discussing the names of your future kids together on your very first date. That's a bit weird, and really isn't appropriate; it could either set up false expectations or rightfully scare them away. Be intentional but not intense.

Dates can still be fun; you should be able to have fun together. But having fun is not the actual goal of dating. It's a side effect, an excuse to get together and have these conversations.

That's why I'm a fan of low-key first dates. I'm not saying you have to do first dates a certain way, but knowing that the overall goal is to get to know each other better, something like a conversation over coffee works well. It's low-cost, avoids undue pressure, and gives you the flexibility to either chat for hours or cordially call it off after twenty minutes. Save the big romantic gestures for when the relationship is serious enough to justify them.

Every date is a green light/yellow light/red light situation. You're looking for information to decide whether you should clearly continue in the relationship with another date (green light), cautiously consider whether you should continue or not (yellow light), or clearly end the relationship (red light). Stack up enough green lights in a row, and voilà, you're married. Hit a red light, and you know you're on the wrong road and need to turn around and move on to someone else. Yellow means you need more information to determine whether the light should be green or red. It's not a deal breaker; most relationships will hit a yellow light. But if you're stuck on yellow for a long while, it might be a sign you're not going anywhere together.

Dating in Community

When you need help making dating decisions—whether it is navigating a yellow light, deciding whether to start dating someone, or deciding to stop dating them—where do you turn for advice? Don't you wish you had help in knowing what to do next?

We've already established that worldly dating advice is mostly worthless. If you are taking your cues from a secular culture where the majority of relationships end badly, then you'd almost be better off doing the opposite of what the world says.

The Bible is the obvious and reliable source of wisdom, but you have to be able to rightly apply it. There is no verse in Habakkuk 4 that says, "And you, (insert your name here), should break up with your girlfriend, for lo, she is not marriageable material."

One thing the Bible is exceedingly clear on, though, is that big decisions should not be made in isolation. To give just a couple of examples, Proverbs 12:15 says, "The way of fools seems right to them, but the wise listen to advice," while Proverbs 15:22 states, "Plans fail for lack of counsel, but with many advisers they succeed."

When we're making important decisions, whether in dating or in any area of life, God wants us to listen to wise counselors. They do have to be *wise* counselors; to quote another proverb, "Walk with the wise and become wise, for a companion of fools suffers harm" (13:20). You know you have wise counselors when they base their advice on God's wisdom as revealed in Scripture.

As a believer, you should be a part of a local church, and through that you should have brothers or sisters in Christ who you spend time with, who know you well, and who care for you and want what is best for you. As a group, they should be able to help you wisely and biblically navigate any dating decisions. You can learn from their past mistakes and successes. They can help you figure out how to date and even who to date. I'm a big fan of having other sets of eyes looking out for you—people who know you well but who also know other believers of the opposite sex and can recommend if there is a godly man or woman out there who would be a good match for you.

When you need help in dating, that is where you should go. If you don't have a community of wise counselors around you, seek them out before you start seeking a spouse.

It's Not Complicated

Don't follow the world and turn dating into this super complicated thing only an expert can figure out. It's not complicated. It's actually so simple. Be honest, be clear, and be intentional. Don't play games, and don't put up with people who do.

In a way, the difficult part of dating is just finding someone else who is not playing games and isn't interested in playing around. Because when two people are both fully committed to following Christ, are ready for a lifelong commitment, and are willing to pursue each other in an intentional, God-honoring way, that kind of relationship is going to be successful 100 percent of the time. Be that kind of person, find that kind of person, and get married already.

8

No Strings Attached

THE LIE: sex in dating is natural, helpful, or even necessary.

THE TRUTH: there is something even better waiting for you if you wait—and full forgiveness is available if you haven't.

The first time I had sex was in the ninth grade.

For a little context, I had been through True Love Waits (a program focused on abstinence and purity). I had signed a written pledge saying that I would abstain from sex until marriage. I had a little gold purity ring, which I wore with pride at my Catholic school and at Baptist youth group meetings.

However, I also started "dating," or at least having girls whom I would call my girlfriends, in the fifth grade. And from fifth grade on, I was never single for more than a week at a time. When I would break up with a girl (or she would break up with me), within a week I would have another girlfriend. Part of the reason for that is because a lot of my relationships were overlapping; I'd already be dating someone else before breaking up with the previous girl (a practice also known as "cheating").

By my freshman year in high school I had a "serious" girlfriend (about as serious as you can have as a freshman). We didn't have sex. But when we broke up, she immediately started dating another guy. She gave me a taste of my own medicine, basically. I felt hurt, but rather than dealing with that hurt, I instead immediately started dating another girl myself. And it was in this new relationship, this heartbroken rebound relationship, that I first had sex. We weren't even serious yet; it happened really early in the relationship, pretty much right off the bat.

I remember crying hysterically that night after I lost my virginity. Looking back now, I don't know exactly why I cried. I don't know if I felt like I'd disappointed my parents, disappointed God, disappointed myself, or if I was just really emotional. But I do remember feeling devastated that night.

However, I continued to date her, and we had sex again. At that point, it was like the door had been opened; we'd already had sex once, so why not again? And as I moved on through other relationships in high school, sex became like a sport to me. It was my main goal of dating.

I took this idea of sex as sport with me to college. Now on my own, as an official adult, I had the full freedom to pursue sex, pornography, and strip clubs. And so, sex in all its forms started to consume my life. It was like the old example of the frog in boiling water: if you put a frog in a pot of hot water, it will immediately (and wisely) hop back out. But if you put a frog in a pot of cool water, it will just float there comfortably. It won't hop out. And if you then turn on the stove and slowly heat that water up, the frog won't notice the gradual change in temperature and will stay in the pot until it has boiled to death. That's sort of what happened to me: because it was gradual, I didn't realize I was becoming completely consumed by sex. I thought it was normal. I was just that fun guy who liked to go to strip clubs, had a ton of porn on his computer, would call in sick to work some days so he could spend the day at home watching porn, always had a girlfriend (or multiple girlfriends, although the girls involved didn't know that), and had sex with as many of them as he could. I went from purity ring to pure sex addict, in a way that would have been unfathomably shocking to me if it had happened all at once, but which I barely even noticed because it happened so gradually.

Fast-forward a couple of years, and I was getting married. My new bride and I had only recently changed our ways and were now following Christ. We said our vows and walked down the aisle together as man and wife. And standing in the chapel foyer after the wedding, I literally prayed to God to thank him for letting me escape the consequences of my sexual sins. Specifically, I thanked him that I didn't have an STD, I didn't have any children out of wedlock, and I didn't have an angry, crazy ex-girlfriend waiting outside to kill me. I thought I had gotten away with it. I thought I had escaped all the consequences of my sexual past.

Well, I was wrong. I hadn't gotten away with it. Even though I had (by complete grace) avoided those obvious consequences, I was not free from scars. The first year of marriage was great; it was the honeymoon period. We went to movies, ate out at restaurants, and just enjoyed each other. But year two was a mess. I had spent all my single years in intensive training for how to *not* be married. I was an expert at how to be promiscuous, unfaithful, and selfish. I was addicted to variety (that's what porn does). I had no idea how to selflessly love a woman; I was used to using women instead. And it caused my marriage to be miserable. I choose that word carefully. It was *miserable*. I realized how foolish I had been, not only in my past promiscuity but in thinking that I had somehow escaped its consequences. At that point, I would have gladly traded consequences; I would have rather had the STD, the child out of wedlock, or the psycho ex than to be trapped in this marriage by vows I couldn't possibly fulfill.

Through God's grace, and with a lot of hard work and forgiveness by both my wife and me, we were able to change and heal and build a marriage that is honestly great today. If you are reading my story and are seeing echoes of your own in it, know that there is hope. It just takes a lot of time and work, and it is not a fun process. And if you're reading this and you haven't made all the bad choices I have, I want to encourage you to learn from my mistakes rather than making your own. Because even if you could avoid the earthly consequences of sexual sin—even if that were possible—it's still not what God has in mind for you. It's not his design and not the way to experience the kind of life he wishes for you.

No Strings Attached

Modern culture treats sex outside of marriage[a] as being no big deal. It's considered completely normal and not something

---

a. I say "outside of marriage" rather than "before marriage" because it is more honest. "Sex before marriage" is only honest if you actually do later get married to the person. If we treated premarital sex with the same seriousness that we treat the other to be ashamed of; if anything, people brag about it and argue that it's a positive good. It's described as being a "casual" activity; something you can do with "no strings attached." You can supposedly have meaningless "hookups," "one-night stands," or text your "friends with benefits" to set up a "booty call," which is probably the most unromantic thing I can even think of.

This idea that sex outside of marriage is OK is probably the biggest lie we are told, and the biggest source of our problems—not just in dating, but in all of life. I know that is a bold statement, but consider the evidence: after the so-called "sexual revolution" of the 1960s, divorce rates doubled, followed by an ongoing decline in marriage rates.[1] Currently, 40 percent of children in the United States are born out of wedlock, without a stable, married, two-parent family; in the 1960s, at the start of the sexual revolution, that number was just 7 percent.[2] Besides those births, there have been 60 million US children killed before birth via abortion since 1973.[3] Sexually transmitted diseases (STDs), which would be almost nonexistent if all people were monogamous,[b] are instead at record highs,[4] with something like 20 million new infections in the country each year.[5] Pornography use has become so common that it's just kind of assumed for men but is also regularly consumed by at least a third of all women.[6] And then you have all the ways people use and abuse sex as a

---

kind of "sex outside of marriage"—adultery—we'd end up with less of both, since premarital sex is a form of training for extramarital sex. And, biblically speaking, we should treat them roughly the same.

b. Although the diseases known as STDs can sometimes be transmitted non-sexually through methods like needle sharing, the actual "sexually transmitted" part would essentially not exist if everyone had no more than one sexual partner—which, in turn, would make STDs so rare that there would be little danger of being infected through other methods.

way to use and abuse other people through either harassment or assault, which is a huge problem: it's estimated that one in five women are raped at some point in their lives,[7] while the majority are either harassed or assaulted in some form.[8]

Go beyond the statistics and think about how all these things would affect the actual people involved, and all the various costs associated with each one. Add it all up, and the impact both on society and on individual relationships is ridiculously massive.

God's Design for Sex

The problem here is not sex. Sex is not a bad thing. It's actually a very good thing. Sex was God's genius invention. He made us male and female. He made our parts and made them fit the way they do. He placed the nerve endings where they are so that sex would feel the way that it does. It is God's creation, and it is good!

The problem is that we stopped following God's design for sex. Sex is designed for marriage. It is wholly unsuited for any other context.

This is apparent when you honestly look at what sex is and what it does.

Sex is the most physically intimate thing you can do with another person. In sex, you are fully exposed, fully vulnerable, and fully connected. That is why, from the very start, sex and marriage were described by God as a man and wife becoming "one flesh."[c] When you get married and when you have sex, the two of you become one unit, one body, which

c. Genesis 2:24: "That is why a man leaves his father and mother and is united to his wife, and they become one flesh."

should no more be separated than half of your body should be cut off.[d]

Scientifically, sex releases hormones that are designed to "rewire" the brain, creating a lasting bond with the person you are with. These hormones, such as oxytocin and vasopressin, make you feel a strong attachment to your sexual partner, while becoming relatively less interested in pursuing another man or woman.[9]

These same hormones are what cause us to bond to our children, which gives an idea of how powerful the bond is—or is supposed to be. When you go against God's design and have sex with multiple people outside of marriage, you are creating bonds with multiple people and then breaking those bonds. That isn't how bonding is supposed to work, and it can affect your ability to truly bond with one person in marriage. Some of the hormones released during sex are basically addictive drugs—natural, healthy chemicals made by your own body, but addictive nonetheless.[10] They can help you become "addicted" to your spouse in a monogamous marriage. But if you are having sex with a series of partners (like I once did), you can just become addicted to sex itself or addicted to having a variety of partners, making it harder to be content and faithful in marriage.

Imagine a piece of tape that has been applied and peeled off, applied and peeled off, again and again. Eventually it will lose its stickiness. It will lose its ability to bond.

Besides bonding, sex is also designed by God as the way we procreate and have children. Again, this is a very good part of God's design; without it our species would cease

d. Matthew 19:6: "So they are no longer two, but one flesh. Therefore what God has joined together, let no one separate."

to exist. However, kids are healthiest, happiest, safest, and most secure when they are raised by both a mother and a father within a committed, stable, God-honoring marriage. Children raised in any type of family other than with their married parents—in other words, single parents, divorced parents, stepparents, or cohabiting couples—are more likely to be poor, more likely to have behavioral or psychological problems, more likely to be abused, and less likely to graduate from high school.[11] Children are a natural outcome of sex, at least part of the time. That's true even if you try to prevent it using birth control, since no form of contraception is 100 percent effective.[12] If you have sex outside of marriage, you are running the risk of having a child outside of marriage, which can be hard for you and for the innocent child.

It's important to note that all of these statistically negative outcomes for children are still far preferable to their death, which is why abortion is not the answer to pregnancy outside of marriage (or inside marriage). But many people decide that abortion is the answer when faced with those circumstances, and the tragedy of having tens of millions of children killed before birth is directly related to the modern prevalence of sex outside of marriage. It's sick that we've twisted something as beautiful and wonderful as pregnancy, where new life is created, and turned it into a negative consequence to be avoided (or "terminated" if we can't avoid it). But that's what happens when we go against God's design. There are consequences, for ourselves and for the people we love.

"No strings attached"? There are always strings. So many strings. But let me clearly say this: I've been very honest about my own poor choices, and I can say from my own experience that God loves you no matter what choices you've made. He is not mad at you. He desires a relationship with you. You do not need to be overwhelmed with shame. You need to receive his grace and forgiveness.

God's Word on Sex

It's for all these reasons (and probably more that I've forgotten to mention) that God calls us to reserve sex for within marriage. His "rules," if you even want to call them that, are simply guidelines to point us toward what is best for us and to help us avoid unnecessary pain.

He's not trying to spoil your fun. Sex is fun, or at least it can be, between two people who are fully committed to lovingly caring for and serving each other. And God created it that way. He didn't really have to make it enjoyable. He made it that way especially for us. I grew up in farm country, around a lot of different kinds of animals. All the animals I know of only have sex for procreation, not recreation. They are only interested in sex during the approximately one time per year they are fertile. God could have made us like that, but he didn't. He made it something we can enjoy, in marriage, with very few limits. If you're married, he *wants* you to enjoy it. And if you're single, he wants you to abstain from sex until you are married, because outside of marriage sex does not bring the joy, freedom, and love you are looking for.

Through most of history, nobody would have really argued with me on these points. Sex and marriage have almost always been linked, to the point where sex outside of marriage could be considered a capital offense. In Old Testament times, you could be stoned to death for having premarital sex or having an affair.[e] But whereas having sex with someone who is not your spouse *after* you get married is still almost universally frowned upon today, having sex with someone who is not your spouse *before* you get married is commonly accepted and expected. In fact, I've often heard people argue in favor of premarital sex as a positive thing, claiming that it is good for you and your relationships. (They're wrong about that; the actual evidence shows that people who wait until marriage to have sex end up with more stable marriages, are more satisfied with the relationship, and are happier with the quality of sex after marriage.[13])

Some Christians make this same claim that premarital sex is OK. They say they believe the Bible, but then try to make it say what they want it to say. Therefore, just to make sure it is clear: the Bible does say that premarital sex is a sin. Besides the whole "worthy of a stoning" thing in the Old Testament, the New Testament is full of warnings against "sexual immorality" (sometimes translated "fornication"). Sexual immorality is different than "adultery," or having sex with someone else after marriage, because both are listed as separate sins in 1 Corinthians 6:9. And in the next chapter, while continuing that discussion, the apostle Paul says that a logical way to avoid giving in to the temptation of "sexual immorality" is to get married and have regular sex with your spouse.[f] He says that "if they [unmarried people] cannot control themselves, they should marry, for it is better to marry than to burn with passion" (1 Cor. 7:9). If premarital sex was at all an acceptable option, then the simple solution for "burning with passion" would be to just have

e. See Deuteronomy 22:13–24 for three examples.
f. See 1 Corinthians 7:1–9.

sex outside of marriage. Logically, premarital sex is not the solution for the temptation to commit sexual immorality because premarital sex *is* sexual immorality. The New Testament also lists "impurity," "debauchery," and "orgies"[g] as sins, just to make it clearer that there are no loopholes.

Pornography and Masturbation (Yup, I'm Going There)

Speaking of loopholes (or the lack thereof), Jesus himself sets the highest standard for sexual purity, saying in Matthew 5:28 that "anyone who looks at a woman lustfully has already committed adultery with her in his heart." He immediately clarifies that in a not-so-subtle way, saying, "If your right eye causes you to stumble, gouge it out and throw it away," and "If your right hand causes you to stumble, cut it off and throw it away" (vv. 29–30). So . . . yeah. He's talking about lust and masturbation. The reason why you don't have a bunch of one-eyed, one-handed Christians running around is because it is understood that he didn't mean it literally; obviously you can still lust with one eye or masturbate with one hand. What he *is* saying is that lust and masturbation are things you should strongly seek to avoid and cut out of your life. This also fits with Paul's instructions in 1 Corinthians 7:9; he also didn't consider masturbation to be a solution to the "burn with passion" problem. According to God's stated standards, these things are still a form of sex outside

g. See Galatians 5:19–21, where it also includes "sexual immorality" and says these are all "obvious" sins, and that "those who live like this will not inherit the kingdom of God."

of marriage: lust is sex with someone else in your heart, and masturbation is sex with yourself. Besides being an awkward thing to talk about (sorry), I know being called to cut out lust and masturbation, especially as a single and celibate person, can feel defeating. I've definitely been there. I can remember, early in my faith journey, hearing a single guy celebrate that he had just had his three-year anniversary of not masturbating. I thought, *Three years? How is that even possible?!* That stuff was such a common part of my life for so long that I didn't know there was such a thing as abstaining from it.

It's also so common, especially with the prevalence of pornography today, that I can't just ignore it in this chapter. Pornography—which is, of course, created solely for the purpose of lust and often fuels masturbation—has been around in some form since ancient times.[14] But today we're living in this giant real-world experiment where, for the first time in history, graphic hardcore video pornography is freely available to just about anyone who wants it, any time they want it, at any age, in the privacy of their own homes. I'm not even sure we fully know the consequences of that yet, but so far studies show that pornography leads to addiction, lower sexual satisfaction, increased loneliness, increased infidelity,[15] and increased divorce.[16]

Again, God isn't trying to steal your fun; he wants what is best for you. Pornography, lust, and masturbation are not at all in your best interest long-term. One of the most loving things you can do for both yourself and your future spouse is to avoid such things, stop doing them, and/or heal from your addiction to them.

I've rarely met an honest man, single or married, who

hasn't struggled with these things at some point in his life. It's a common problem for women too, but it's more common and more frequent with men.[17] There are a few men who have never intentionally looked at pornography, but they are sadly in the minority. And, also sadly, I am not in that minority. In fact, even though I talk about the subject publicly and therefore have talked with a lot of men who are addicted to pornography, I don't think I've ever met anyone who struggles with it worse than I did when I was younger. I'm not saying that I'm uniquely *the* worst; I just haven't met anyone who is decidedly more of an addict than I was. And that should give you hope; if it's possible for me to change, it is possible for you to do so as well.

If you struggle with pornography and don't know how to stop, one of the biggest keys (for me, and for just about everyone else I know who's overcome such an addiction) is to simply remove access. If that means getting rid of your personal computer or smartphone, so be it. ("If your right eye causes you to stumble, gouge it out and throw it away.") It may just mean installing good software that blocks questionable content (and turning over the controls for such software to someone else, so you can't disable it).

Another key is to pray. Every morning, I would pray for God's help in keeping my eyes and thoughts pure. I knew I needed his help.

Finally, one of the ways God does help is through his church and the provision of like-minded community. Don't go at it alone; find others to help. Christ-centered addiction recovery programs such as re:generation (regenerationrecovery.org) or Celebrate Recovery (celebraterecovery.com) can help; find one in your area.

Remember that none of this is meant to shame you. Of course we've all sinned; that's why we need Jesus's sacrifice on the cross to pay for our sins. But I want to encourage you to seek out a better way.

How Far Is Too Far?

Let's say that you are in a relationship, but you're committed to dating with purity and saving sex until after you are married. It's natural enough to wonder, How far is too far? Physically, where are the lines you should not cross?

I get that question a lot, but I think it's the wrong one to be asking. It's literally saying, "How close can I get to sin without actually sinning?" But the goal is not to get as close to sin as possible; it should be to stay as far away from sin as possible.

It's like someone is standing on the roof of a building and asking, "How close can I get to the edge?" My response to that would be, Why do you want to get close to the edge? Is it because you want to jump off? If you desire to jump off, then you really need to come down off the roof completely, before you get hurt.

First Corinthians 6:18 says, "Flee from sexual immorality." *Flee* from it. That doesn't sound like getting as close to it as you can without actually crossing the line. It sounds more like turning around and running as fast as you can in the opposite direction.

In practice, this means your goal in dating should not be to simply avoid going "too far." It means you shouldn't even start down the path toward having sex until you've first walked down the aisle. If you find yourself heading that direction, you should stop and back off.

Instead of getting as close as you can to sin, get as close as you can to holiness.

Sexual Compatibility

What about the need to make sure you and your potential spouse are "sexually compatible" before marriage?

"Sexual compatibility" is another lie told by society. Physically, we're not talking USB vs. coaxial cable here. If you take any random man and any random woman and put them together on a deserted island, let's just say that life would go on. The pieces would be compatible, if they chose to come together in that way.

In terms of so-called chemistry, I'm sure you can tell whether you are attracted to someone without actually having sex. If anything, if you have to try it out to tell if there is "chemistry" there, that's probably a good sign there isn't.

Really, it comes back to what I've said previously about compatibility: no two people are truly compatible. In marriage, you have to learn how to work together and selflessly serve each other. With God's Spirit in them,[h] any two people can choose to do this, and it's that (and only that) which can make you compatible, whether in the bedroom or outside of it.

It's actually the "outside the bedroom" part you should be more focused on. Because, for starters, how you love and serve each other outside the bedroom will be the biggest determinant of how things go inside the bedroom. That's another thing society gets wrong: sex is about far more than just what happens between the sheets.

h. Galatians 5:22–23 says that "the fruit of the Spirit is love, joy, peace, forbearance, kindness, goodness, faithfulness, gentleness and self-control."

The other reason why "sexual compatibility" isn't a thing to test out before marriage is because marriage isn't about sex. Based on estimates for how often married people have sex and how long those encounters probably last, the average married couple spends somewhere around 0.625 percent of their time having sex.[18] Which means you spend 99.375 percent of your time together in marriage doing other things. Maybe you think you'll be above average in terms of how often you have sex; maybe you can even *double* the average. Great. Good for you. But that still means you'll have sex a whopping 1.25 percent of the time.

As far as tiny percentages go, it's an important 0.625 percent (or 1.25 percent, you overachiever) of your future marriage. But it's not the focus of marriage, just like it shouldn't be the focus of your life. If you want a good marriage, you'd better work on preparing for that other 99 percent instead. And one way to do that is to not make your dating relationship about sex. You'll have a lifetime to figure out the 1 percent together, but only if your relationship has a solid foundation that is not based on sex.

Start Now

I know that most people—a really high percentage—do have sex before they get married. Which means it is likely that most people reading this also fit in that category.

If that describes you, please know there is no judgment here. I bought the lies too. And God is not surprised when people don't follow his ways. *Everyone* fails to live up to God's perfect standard; this just happens to be one of the most common ways people fail.

God will forgive you, if you want to be forgiven. First John 1:9 says, "If we confess our sins, he is faithful and just and will forgive us our sins and purify us from all unrighteousness." You can be pure in God's sight.

However, along with confession and forgiveness should come repentance. *Repentance* means you sincerely acknowledge that what you did was wrong, and you therefore seek to change your ways and not do that thing again.[i] It's possible to still fail at times, but repentance means it's your sincere desire to not fail in that way.

When Jesus started preaching, the very first recorded word out of his mouth was "Repent" (Matt. 4:17). And the famous line often translated as "Go and sin no more" specifically comes from Jesus confronting a person caught in sexual sin, in John 8:11: "'Then neither do I condemn you,' Jesus declared. 'Go now and leave your life of sin.'"

Confess, be forgiven, but then change your ways. If you are living in sexual sin (or any sin) there is nothing preventing you from changing right now; today can be the day you change your ways.

Forgiveness means that God will no longer hold your sins against you, in any way, and you will not have to face the eternal consequences of your sins. However, there can be natural earthly consequences of sexual sin, and those cannot all be avoided. You may already be living in those consequences, or (as in my case) there may be consequences that only become fully clear later on. There may be a grieving process for mistakes you've made, but there doesn't have to be any shame. There is a difference; as 2 Corinthians 7:10

---

i. Acts 26:20 says that people "should repent and turn to God and demonstrate their repentance by their deeds."

says, "Godly sorrow brings repentance that leads to salvation and leaves no regret, but worldly sorrow brings death." You can avoid worldly sorrow by trusting that "there is now no condemnation for those who are in Christ Jesus" (Rom. 8:1) and "if anyone is in Christ, the new creation has come: The old has gone, the new is here!" (2 Cor. 5:17). You are not defined by your old self; just commit to truly making it your "old" self.

Talking about Your Past

If you have had sex in the past and are now dating someone else, at some point you will need to confess that to them and ask for their forgiveness. You also have to be willing to forgive them for their past.

This is not a first-date conversation, but it is one you need to have at some point before marriage. There should be no secrets in marriage; they have the right to know about your past, even if you are now a different person.

A word of caution, though: although you have the *right* to know everything about your spouse's past, you don't *need* to know all of the details, and in fact you might not *want* to. I doubt it will make your marriage better if you know every tiny detail of their sexual past, or if they know every tiny detail about yours. And once you do learn something, it can't be unlearned; you have to live with that knowledge. Therefore, don't ask your future spouse for any details you might regret knowing, and don't burden them with any details they haven't asked for. If they want to know, you should answer honestly, but both of you should be careful what you ask for.

When Monica and I were dating, I did want to know every detail about her past. I don't think that knowledge has helped me in marriage at all, and I kind of wish I'd never asked. For her part, Monica didn't really want to know about my past, even though I had a much more extensive history than she did. That's her choice, and I think it was a wise one.

Be Different

I know that what God is calling us to here is countercultural in the extreme. Today's culture makes fun of virginity. Hollywood makes comedy movies entirely based on the seemingly absurd idea of *not* having sex.[j] If you commit to God's way, there will be those who don't understand. Some people will think you're crazy. Remaining pure may even cost you a relationship or two with people who think sex is a necessary part of dating (in which case, you can be thankful you've successfully dodged a bullet).

But we are called to be different. We are to "not conform to the pattern of this world" (Rom. 12:2). We are to be "children of God without fault in a warped and crooked generation" who "shine among them like stars in the sky" (Phil. 2:15).

So be different. Even if it were possible to avoid all the consequences of sexual sin—it's not, but even if it were—we should still strive to follow God's design for sex and marriage. We should do so both because it is his design and also because it is different. It's an opportunity to reclaim his world from fallen culture and serve as a living example that he makes people new. Start today. Be different.

j. For example, *The 40-Year-Old Virgin* and *40 Days and 40 Nights*.

9

Try It before You Buy It

THE LIE: living together is the best way to prepare for marriage.

THE TRUTH: marriage is permanent, so unless you are practicing permanence, you're not preparing for marriage.

A friend of mine was helping his fiancée move into a new apartment, just six weeks before their wedding date. It was the apartment they would soon be sharing as a married couple, and like any good fiancé (who also happened to own a truck), he volunteered to serve her in that way.

It seemed like a common enough thing. It was a large apartment complex, and there was probably someone new moving in just about every day. However, the leasing manager who handled all of those move-ins was baffled. Why? Because, although my friend was helping his fiancée move in, he wasn't moving in with her. That would have to wait six weeks, until after they were married. The fact that they were waiting until marriage to move in together was something the leasing manager couldn't quite comprehend. Even more confusing to this manager was the fact that my friend's own lease ended in *five* weeks, not six; he was going to move into somebody else's guest bedroom for a week before moving into their new apartment. It would have been far easier to just move in with her then, but they were both committed to waiting until they were married to start living together.

Up until a generation or two ago, the idea of living with your boyfriend or girlfriend without being married to them would have been almost unthinkable. It would have been shocking. Nowadays, cohabitation has become so common that it's almost shocking when people *don't* live together before marriage. Just to show how drastically things have changed: for young adults ages twenty-five to thirty-four, cohabitation is now *seventy-four times* more common than it was fifty years ago. For people ages eighteen to twenty-four, it is *ninety-four times* more common.[1] Today, about two-thirds of married couples have lived together with someone, though not necessarily their spouse, before walking down the aisle.[2]

This is a complete seismic shift in how people think about dating and relationships. We've reordered the steps. Instead of "Get ready, get set, go!" it's now "Get ready, go, get set!" The main things that used to define being married—living together and having sex—now typically come before the commitment of marriage.

Think about how meaningless this makes some of our most cherished and romanticized traditions. "You may now kiss the bride"—you're being given permission to kiss, yet you've already done far more than that. Carrying your new bride over the threshold—to the place you've already been living together for three years. Going on a honeymoon to celebrate and consummate your new life together—something that is now so unexciting and unremarkable that some couples spend the time apart on separate solo vacations known as "unimoons."[3] I'm reminded of another friend who attended a wedding where the couple was already living together, and afterward the groom invited him to go fishing that night. It was his wedding night, and he wanted to spend it fishing with other guys in the pond out back.

Practically Married

The main argument in favor of living together is that, although it may not be romantic, it's practical. It's the "try it before you buy it" mindset. By cohabitating, you are living as if you were already married. According to this logic, living together serves as a trial run for marriage. If it goes well, you can get married and be confident that your marriage will be successful.

I can understand how this seems to logically make sense. Sure, it goes against the biblical model of marriage and openly flaunts the sin of premarital sex, but let's say for the sake of argument that you don't care about that. (A lot of people don't.) In that case, cohabitation would make sense, right?

That's what I find so interesting about this topic. Although it seems like cohabitation should be good practice for marriage, and that people who live together first should therefore have more successful marriages, statistically *the opposite is true.* As many studies have consistently shown over time, people who live together before marriage are more likely to divorce.[4] They experience less satisfaction in marriage, spend less time together, are less dedicated to their marriage, and are less confident about its success.[5] They also experience higher rates of negative communication, adultery, and domestic violence.[6] Basically, when you cohabitate first, everything you want to go up in marriage goes down, and everything you want to go down goes up.

Ending Marriage before It Starts

All of that, of course, assumes that you actually do get married to the person you are living with. But that is often not the case.

If cohabitation was truly a precursor to marriage, then you would expect the huge increase in cohabitation rates to also lead to higher marriage rates. But the opposite has happened: in the past fifty years, the percentage of young adults ages twenty-five to thirty-four who are married has fallen by half. In 1968, 81 percent of all people in that age range were married; now it is only 40 percent.[7] For people ages eighteen to twenty-four, the number of married couples has dropped from 39 percent to just 9 percent.[8]

That's because cohabitation isn't a precursor to marriage; it's a replacement for marriage. It removes most of the motivation for getting married. This is especially true for men; whereas women often think of cohabitation as a positive step toward marriage, the men they are living with are less likely to have marriage as an end goal.[9] It's a classic example of the old saying, "Why buy the cow when you can get the milk for free?" If someone is only interested in sex and shared rent, and they are already getting those things from you without having to commit to anything, why would they get married and limit their options?

The fact is, only about half of all cohabiting couples ever do get married.[10] That means, barring a few people who stay in living together limbo but never make it official through marriage, about half of all cohabiting couples eventually break up. But because your lives are so entangled, breaking up with someone you are living with is almost as complicated and painful as a divorce. At least one of you has to find a new place to live. You have to divide up shared belongings or assets. You may have kids you have to figure out custody for; almost one in five cohabiting couples becomes pregnant within one year of moving in together.[11] This problem with breaking up is a fact that's conveniently ignored by everyone who tries to defend cohabitation. Even if the divorce rate and all the other marital statistics were the same—they're not, but even if they were—then cohabitation would still be a terrible idea, because you have a 50 percent chance of your pretend marriage ending in a way that closely resembles a very real divorce. When you add the 50 percent chance of "divorce" before you even get married to the increased chance of divorce for the cohabitators who do get married, you'll see that living together is the best way to practically ensure you'll experience that kind of pain.

Why Living Together Doesn't Work

If it seems like living together should be good practice or a "trial run" for marriage, why doesn't it work out that way?

For starters, obviously the idea that living together somehow helps you get ready for marriage is a misconception. Just because you are living together does not in any way mean you are actively preparing for marriage together. It is entirely possible to live together and not truly get to know each other in a deep way, or not take the time to discuss anything of importance. For example, I know one woman who got married just a few months ago after living with her boyfriend for several years. Soon afterward, she was complaining to friends about their financial situation; her husband had huge amounts of debt he had never mentioned to her before the wedding. If they had been less focused on being together physically in the present and more focused on actually talking to each other and preparing for a future together, they would have a much healthier marriage today.

Also, although roughly half of all couples who live together break up before marriage, there are also many others who get married when they should have broken up. As I've just mentioned, when you live together for very long, the costs of breaking up become very high. It's almost as difficult as a divorce. That means it actually becomes easier to get married than to break up. People end up getting married not because they are committed to staying together no matter what but because they're taking the path of least resistance. They passively slide into marriage instead of actively deciding to commit.[12]

Speaking of commitment, marriage is supposed to be permanent. The essence of marriage is permanence. And it is impossible to "practice" permanence; you're either committed to staying together or you're not. If you are practicing something that doesn't have that level of commitment, you're not practicing for marriage. You are practicing for something else.

164

But the most obvious reason why cohabitation doesn't work is because, in doing so, you are ignoring God's design for marriage. It is a pretty safe assumption that if you are living with your boyfriend or girlfriend, you are also sleeping together, so see everything in the previous chapter about premarital sex. But it goes beyond sex; the biblical example of marriage involved the groom first going to prepare a place to live with his bride, and then coming back to announce that the place was ready and that the wedding could therefore begin.[13] The wedding date and the move-in date were the same. And God intends this to serve as a picture of what he does for us. That's why Jesus said he was going "to prepare a place for [us]" (John 14:2), he will come back like a bridegroom when the time is right (Matt. 25:1–13), and there will be a wedding celebration when we do go to live with him in paradise (Rev. 19:6–10). When we subvert or ignore that model of marriage, we are missing out on the experience God wants for us. We are choosing something that is less than God's best.

I've said before that two people who are both fully committed to following Christ will always have a successful marriage, because they will selflessly serve each other, consistently work together to resolve conflict, forgive each other for small offenses, and avoid intentionally doing things that will hurt the other. But two people who are living together before marriage are, by definition, both not fully following Christ. It is therefore no surprise that they would have more problems in marriage.

It's almost like God knows what he is talking about,[a] and you should trust the One who created marriage to know what is best for you.

a. Sarcasm intended.

What If You're Not Having Sex?

When I talk to groups of singles about cohabitation, I always get at least a few objections. One of the most common questions I get is, "What if I'm living with my boyfriend/girlfriend, but we're not having sex?"

I would say that is still an extremely bad idea, for three reasons.

The first problem is that you're unnecessarily setting yourself up for temptation. It's almost like you want the maximum temptation possible, even though your goal is to not give in. That's not wise.

The second problem is that you are training yourself to live with this person and not have sex. That's not a good habit to get into if or when you do get married. Habits are hard to break, and that can be a difficult mental switch to flip. You may find yourself married but still not having sex, because that's what you have trained for.

Finally, there's the problem of how it looks to outsiders. Most people, when they hear someone is living with their significant other, will just assume the couple is also having sex. It gives the appearance you are doing that, even if you are not. And that's going to be confusing to people, if you say you're a Christian but also imply you have no problem with having sex outside of marriage. The Bible encourages us to live "above reproach" (1 Tim. 3:2) and says we should stand out as being different from those who don't know God, "[shining] among them like stars in the sky" (Phil. 2:15). You're missing out on a chance to witness to a world that desperately needs some good examples of how to live wisely and marry well.

What If We're Already Engaged?

Another question I get is whether it is OK to live together if you are already engaged.

This one is a bit confusing to me. If you're engaged, it means you've already decided to get married. You don't want to wait to start living together as a couple? So why don't you just get married already? It solves both problems at once.

God doesn't command you to have a big wedding that takes months or years to plan. He does want you to wait until marriage before living as though you were married. If you are going to compromise somewhere, compromise on the one-time party that lasts just a few hours. Don't compromise on God's commands or cheapen the lifelong adventure that is marriage.

What If We Can't Afford to Live Separately?

It is true that sharing a place to live saves money. You only have one rent or mortgage payment a month, instead of two. Financially, that can be a big deal.

However, there is absolutely no reason why you have to live with your boyfriend or girlfriend in order to enjoy those savings. You can save just as much money by having a roommate. In fact, I often encourage singles to have a roommate (or two, or three). Not only does it save you money but it can teach you how to compromise and get along with someone else in a shared space.

Whatever reason you may try to come up with for why you should live with your boyfriend or girlfriend—I've heard them all by now, and they are all just excuses to justify doing what you want to do, in direct opposition to what God says to do. Don't come up with excuses for sin. Trust that God knows and wants what is best for you.

Dating from a Distance

While cohabitation has been on the rise, the number of long-distance relationships also seems to be increasing.[14] In a way, the fact that long-distance relationships can work at all is yet another indictment of the cohabitation myth. After all, the two are essentially opposites. Instead of physically being under the same roof every day, long-distance daters are rarely even in the same city together. And yet I can think of many people in successful marriages now who dated long-distance for at least some period of time—my wife and I included.

The reason long-distance dating can work is because it forces you to talk to each other. If you are together physically, it is easy to mistakenly build a relationship on physical affection. You can feel close to the other person just because you are literally close to them, not because you know them well. But if you want to feel close to someone in a long-distance relationship, you are going to have to actually communicate with them. Technology makes that much easier these days, which is probably why such relationships have become more common.

But this doesn't mean having a long-distance relationship is inherently better than dating someone locally; distance brings its own challenges. For one thing, it is harder to observe each other's lives. You are only seeing what they want you to see. You know how they interact with you but not how they treat the other people in their lives. Figure out what you need to learn about each other before moving forward into marriage, and then figure out a way you each can learn those things.

There are also practical considerations. Although long-distance dating is fine for a time, eventually you do need to be together for the relationship to work. I would not recommend a long-distance marriage; although I know there are circumstances where that can become a necessity for a time, it does not seem healthy and is not something to actively seek out. So, in your long-distance relationship, there needs to be a plan for how and when it would become a short-distance relationship. At least one of you will have to move, likely also changing jobs in the process, so there will be sacrifices to be made. And, while dating, you need to be wise during any times you are able to visit each other in person, due to the temptation that can come from having spent an extended time apart. Don't spend the night at their place and therefore "live together" for the weekend; the cost of a separate Airbnb or hotel room is well worth it. My heart is not to be legalistic here, it's to help you pursue holiness and avoid even the appearance of evil (1 Thess. 5:22).

You can make long-distance dating work; just know that it does require effort and coming up with a solid plan for where the relationship is going.

Ready or Not

As with every area in which we get things wrong, there is forgiveness available if you have lived with someone you are dating outside of marriage, or if you are currently doing so. However, now is the perfect time to change. I'm not saying you have to break up, necessarily, but you really should move out. It is what honors God and what will work out best for you long-term.

My kids, especially when they were little, would sometimes "play house." They would pretend to be married to each other (or to a friend, or to Monica or myself) and have a family of dolls to take care of together. It's cute when you're five. But it's childish when you're twenty-five. Real adults don't pretend. They listen to wise counsel and make wise decisions; they don't just drift through life and take the path of least resistance. They delay gratification until the time is right. They make real commitments and stick to them.

It really boils down to this: if you are dating someone, you're either ready to get married to each other or you're not. If you are ready, get married. Don't buy the lie that you should do a trial run by living together; that's a sign you are not ready and not really committed to making marriage work "for better or worse." If, on the other hand, you're not ready to marry each other, the last thing you should be doing is living together as though you were married. It's a bad practice I want to save you from. It's also an opportunity to show the world you are different, and your first love is Christ.

10

Breaking Up Is Hard to Do

THE LIE: broken hearts are a necessary evil in dating.

THE TRUTH: the heartbreak caused by breaking up can be mostly avoided.

I hid in the bathroom, quite literally beating my head against the wall while ugly-snot-crying. The girl I loved had broken up with me. It seemed that for the rest of my life it would all be downhill from here. I would compare every girl from here on out to Ashley,[a] and they would all come up short. I was doomed, and rather pathetic.

Eventually, I managed to pull myself together enough to go out and face the world again. I wiped my nose, dried my eyes, and walked out of the bathroom—just in time for my sixth-grade science class.

That was my first hard breakup, but there were many more to come. Since I was a serial dater, even from that young age, I've broken up with a lot of girls and had a lot of girls break

a. Names changed to protect privacy.

up with me. Every situation was different, but someone always ended up hurt. There was the popular girl I took whitewater rafting and accidentally hit in the eye with my oar; she later dumped me overboard for another guy. Melanie cheated on me with my best friend; that hurt. But that was only after Molly cheated on my best friend with me; she later left me for someone else. I even broke up with my wife multiple times before we got married.

Breakups are a necessary reality for almost everyone. That's because every dating relationship eventually ends with one of just two outcomes: you either get married or break up. So, unless you marry the first person you date,[b] you will have to experience a breakup at some point. And if you are going to break up, you might as well do it right.

Unfortunately, this is another thing our generation is notoriously bad at. We don't do a good job of ending relationships. We break up by fighting; we break up by cheating; we break up via text. We come up with lame excuses: "It's not you; it's me" (even though it's probably you), or "You're too good for me" (um . . . thanks?), or "I just need some space" (you mean like a larger apartment, or what?). We sometimes try to avoid conflict by avoiding breaking up, even though we know we should. Worst of all, we are the generation that invented "ghosting," which is the most cowardly and cruel way to break up with someone. (If I'm talking to you, STOP IT!)

These bad breakups have consequences, mostly in the form of a lot of hurt, bitter people. We end up with "evil

---

b. It's great if you do. I've heard people argue that it's a bad idea, but I disagree; if you're both mature believers and are willing to commit to each other for life, there is nothing wrong with marrying the first person you date. It's a gift to never have to experience a breakup. It's just that it's also somewhat rare.

exes," or the "psycho ex" we have to block all contact with. We have rebound relationships that are doomed from the start, because they are really all about our ex, not the new person we are with. Or, on the opposite end of the spectrum, we refuse to create any new relationships because we fear the pain of a potential breakup. We mope and cry and lie in bed listening to sad breakup songs. There are even big-time music careers built entirely on the pain of the singer's last breakup; the most successful ones manage to split up with someone new in time for the next album.

It doesn't have to be this way. Breaking up doesn't have to be so hard to do. Part of the problem is how we date, which is why I've talked about not building relationships on feelings, living together, or bonding to someone through sex outside of marriage. All of these things make leaving the relationship much harder. But how you go about breaking up also makes a huge difference.

I'm not saying breakups should be fun, but they don't have to define your life. It's possible to break up with someone (or have them break up with you) and actually be grateful for the experience. And not just in an "I'm stronger because I survived" kind of way. Ending a relationship can be a good thing, and it can be done in a good way.

But before we get to *how* you should break up, you first have to decide whether you should break up at all.

When You Should Break Up

I've mentioned this before, but if the end goal of dating is marriage, then you should break up with someone as soon as you know you're not going to marry them.

I'm not talking about doubt or uncertainty. It's fine if you don't yet know whether or not you are going to marry them; the point of dating is figuring that out. After all, if you already knew that you were going to marry the person, we should be talking about engagement, not dating. What I am saying is that if you are relatively sure you are never going to marry them, or there is some reason you should not marry them, you should break up.

Perhaps I should add the word *now* to that statement. If the relationship is not heading toward marriage, you should break up *now*. One of the ways people tend to get this wrong is that they delay breaking up. They might try to wait for the ideal time or place to break up (whatever that would be). Or, because it's a hard conversation and they don't like feeling uncomfortable, they procrastinate and put it off indefinitely. But the best time to do it is truly *now*. That's because the other person might see the relationship differently. They may think the relationship is going great and that they *are* moving toward marriage with you. Every date you go on, and every day that goes by with the two of you still together, just adds to their excitement and their certainty that this relationship is going to last. The longer you wait to tell them the relationship is *not* going to last, the harder that news will be for them to take. By trying to let them down easy, you inadvertently make it harder.

Why You Should Break Up

As for how you can know that you should not marry them, the number one reason is if one of you is not committed to fully following Christ. That is the "unequally yoked" problem

174

from 2 Corinthians 6:14 (see our discussion of compatibility in chapter 6).

You should break up if the person you are dating is not fully devoted to following Christ. This will be apparent by what they talk about, what they focus their life on, and how they behave, which includes how they treat you (and the other people around them). If they say one thing with their lips but their actions say something different, believe their actions. Some people know all the right answers and can "talk the talk," but it is all a con—sometimes one they are even playing on themselves. A person's actions over time will show what they truly believe.

One obvious example of this is whether they are committed to purity in your relationship. If someone is willing to have sex with you outside of marriage, they are clearly not committed to following God, because they are actively disobeying his commands. They are saying, by their actions, that they don't really fear God. They follow their own desires; that is their god.

You should break up if *either* of you is not following God. That includes you, not just the person you are dating. Really, dating or marriage should be of little concern to you if you don't have your eternal destination figured out. The smart thing to do would be to work on your relationship with the One who offers eternal life and who loves you more than any imperfect human ever could.

Single-Issue Disqualifiers

Because all people are imperfect, there are some faults you'll have to forgive and minor problems you'll have to deal with.

If you called it quits at the first sign of imperfection, none of your relationships would ever make it very far.

However, there are some red flags you cannot afford to overlook. Think of them as single-issue disqualifiers; no matter how great the person may seem to be otherwise, you should still break up with them, because these are problems you absolutely do not want to bring into your future marriage.

It's one thing if someone has dealt with these problems in the past but has since found recovery and freedom from their struggles. If they are a new creation (2 Cor. 5:17), you don't have to hold these things against them. I'm an example; there are things that would have disqualified me at one point, but through God's grace I was able to change and no longer be defined by who I once was. Just be sure they really have changed, as evidenced by a prolonged period of faithfulness.

I am also not saying that these are automatic disqualifiers for a one-time offender. They might be; it depends on the situation. This is another reason why it is important to have others you can go to for advice who know and understand the relationship.

But if someone's life is currently defined by one of these things as an ongoing problem, then that person is disqualified. The best way you can love such a person is to encourage them to get well—by breaking it off until or unless they get well. Don't enable them.

There are three As that are disqualifiers. The first one is *addiction* to any substance. Being an addict doesn't mean you are a terrible person but it does often mean you are terrible to be around when your mind is distorted by the effects of alcohol or other drugs. Before you consider committing your life to such a person, think of how many stories you've heard of people married to alcoholics where the situation ended badly. Now try to think of any story—even one— where being married to an addict was a positive thing. I'm waiting.

The second disqualifier is *anger*. Anyone can get briefly and mildly angry on occasion. But I'm talking about people whose lives are marked by anger. Rather than controlling their temper, they let their temper control them. If they go into a rage when things don't go their way, that is a big red flag. If he (or she) is yelling at you, throwing stuff, or putting hands on you in anger, run. Get out immediately. There should be a one-strike rule in dating: if they strike you once, it's over. Pay attention to this one, because your life could literally depend on it. I don't think people would willingly make the choice to marry an abuser, but they do sometimes make the choice to marry someone with a known anger problem, not realizing that anger problem is likely to turn into abuse soon after.

There was once a couple who was about to get married at my church. Just a few days before the wedding, we learned the groom had an abusive history. There was no evidence he had dealt with the problem; he had just run from it and hidden it. We reached out to his fiancée and asked her if she knew about that aspect of his past. Her reply was, "I didn't know that, but I don't even know if that's true. I think I know the real him." We advised her, "We really think you should delay this wedding, at least to do a little bit more research before moving forward."

To say she was unhappy with us would be an understatement. "I don't want to talk to you guys anymore. Get out of our business. You don't understand. You're just not for us." She took their wedding to a different location, outside the church, and got married on schedule. Not too long after the honeymoon, he threw her through a wall, broke her arm, and fractured her face. It's a tragic story. We were there afterward to help her pick up the pieces of her life. We mourned with her; this wasn't an "I told you so" situation. But I am telling this story to you now so you can learn from it.

To keep the A theme going, the third disqualifier is *adultery*. Now, you could object that technically someone can't commit adultery until after they are married. However, they can do things now that would count as adultery if you were married. That's basically them letting you know they think adultery is no big deal, and that they are likely to continue doing those things after marriage. After all, habits don't magically change when someone walks down the aisle; they are still the same person and are prone to doing the same things. If someone cheats on you now, sexually or otherwise, that is the best possible predictor they would also cheat on you after marriage. You should almost thank them (as you break up with them) for letting you know now that they are an adulterer, before you made the mistake of marrying them.

Looking at pornography is also cheating. It is adultery in your heart, according to Jesus in Matthew 5:28. I often get emails that say, "My boyfriend is looking at porn. What do I do?" As I'm a former porn addict myself, here's what I read when I see that: "My boyfriend is cheating on me repeatedly with many different women. What do I do?" The answer to that question is a bit more obvious: you break up. You let them heal and get well, so they can later enter marriage without bringing that problem along with them.

A person can also clearly show you that they are OK with having sex with someone who is not their spouse by sleeping with (or trying to sleep with) someone who is not their spouse: you. If you haven't married them yet, then you are not their spouse. It doesn't matter how much you may hope to be married to them someday, or what plans you have made together. Even if you are engaged and have a wedding date set, you are still not married until that date. By sleeping together now, you are not respecting the importance of marriage. And practically speaking, until you say those vows, you don't know for certain you are going to marry each other. Either of you could call it off, right up to the last minute. So you're not just getting an early start; you are sleeping with someone who is not your spouse and may never become your spouse. You're both cheating on your future spouses with each other.

You might notice, with all of these disqualifiers, that it really comes back to the overall concept of only marrying someone who is following Christ. If someone is having sex outside of marriage, they are not obeying the Bible's commands about sex. If someone is controlled by anger, they are not following God's commands to be "slow to become angry, because human anger does not produce the righteousness that God desires" (James 1:19–20). And if they are addicted to alcohol or drugs, they are not living out the call to avoid drunkenness (Eph. 5:18), to be self-controlled (Gal. 5:22–23), and to have a sober mind (1 Pet. 4:7; 5:8).

Ignore the Sunk Costs

When deciding whether to break up with someone, you have to ignore the sunk costs. "Sunk cost" is a business term; it refers to the investment you've already made in a project and which you won't be able to get back (because it's already been paid). In dating, there can be a huge sunk cost of emotional investment and time spent together as a couple. You may think, *If we break up, all of that time and effort I've put into the relationship will go to waste.* But that's the thing: it's already gone to waste. By continuing a relationship that is not going anywhere worthwhile, you're just adding to those sunk costs. It's understandable to be sad about what the relationship has cost you, but the best way to limit that cost is to end it and move on.

How You Should Break Up

Once you've decided you should break up, how do you go about doing so the right way?

There are no magical words to say, especially since each situation can be vastly different. But there are a number of principles that apply in all situations.

- **Tell the truth.** When you break up with someone, tell them why. Don't leave them wondering what went wrong or what, if anything, they could have done differently. If there is something about themselves they need to work on, the kind thing to do is to let them know so they don't keep on making the same mistakes. Being silent about the reasons doesn't help them, and neither does making up excuses.
- **Don't shift blame.** The decision is yours. In particular, and this might just be a pet peeve of mine, don't blame God for your breakup. Don't drag him into it and give them a reason to be upset at him just so they won't be as upset at you. God probably didn't

tell you to break up with them. Even if he did, you don't have to blame him. And if you're doing it to obey his command to not be yoked together with an unbeliever, that's not God telling you to break up; that's God saying you shouldn't have been dating an unbeliever in the first place. The responsibility for the relationship still rests on your shoulders.

• **Provide clarity.** Leaders remove confusion, and there should be no confusion over where the two of you now stand. I've talked about "defining the relationship"; this is defining the end of the relationship. If there is something one of you needs to work on, and there is the possibility of getting back together once you are both recovered or healed, you can tell them that, but don't make any promises you can't keep. If it's fully over, then leave no doubt. Quote Taylor Swift if you need to: "We are never, ever, ever getting back together."

• **Tell them in person, if possible.** Part of being clear in communication is communicating face-to-face. If that's not possible due to distance, the next best way is a phone call (or video call). Do *not* break up by text; that is cowardly and often unclear. And no ghosting; that has to be the worst possible way to break up. It's not even technically breaking up. If the other person can't tell whether you are breaking up with them or if you are just dead, that is the opposite of being clear. If they are not sure whether you've broken up or not, you did it all wrong.

• **Don't wait.** If you are waiting for the perfect time to break up, the perfect time is now.

- **Be loving.** Just because you are splitting up doesn't mean you can't be loving toward them and seek what is best for them. Jesus says to love even your enemies and "do good to those who hate you" (Luke 6:27), so no matter the circumstances, that is how you are to treat your ex. Part of being loving is being honest, but you can be honest without being mean. Try to be gentle but firm.
- **Seek peace.** If you have wronged them, seek forgiveness. If they have wronged you, confront them about it and offer forgiveness. There's a chance they might not be willing to forgive you or to admit they need to ask for your forgiveness, but that's out of your control. You just take care of your part. As it says in Romans 12:18, "If it is possible, as far as it depends on you, live at peace with everyone."

Depending on the situation, it may or may not be wise to be friends with an ex. Sometimes it is better for your heart (or their heart) if you don't spend time around them after ending the dating relationship. You have to use judgment there. However, barring that consideration, it should be *possible* for you to still be friends because of the clear and loving way you broke up and the way you sought reconciliation for any hurts or wrongs that happened between the two of you.

Leave Them Better Than You Found Them

Healthy breakups start early in the relationship. Here's what I mean by that: it's not that you are preparing to break up from the start but just that you are dating the right way throughout the relationship. You are seeking what is best for each other at all times and avoiding the mistakes that lead to messy breakups.

Sometimes, for ministry retreats or other events, I've had the privilege to use someone else's place for the weekend. It might be a small private lake house or a camp that hosts a thousand people at once. Regardless, there's a principle I always try to follow and encourage other people using the facility to follow: to leave the place better than we found it. This means that, when we leave, the place will be cleaner than it was when we arrived. If something was broken, we fix it. We take out the trash, we make sure everything is in its place, and we leave a thank-you note.

I think that's a great principle to use in dating as well. Make it your goal to leave the other person better than you found them. Not that it's your goal to leave them at all, but if it doesn't work out and you do have to break up, you want them to be better off because of the experience.

When that's your goal, you date differently from the start. You don't play games or play on their emotions. You are honest with them, and clear on where you think the relationship is or isn't going at all times. You don't go too far with them physically, or do anything that might leave them with additional baggage. If there's an area they need to grow in, or perhaps some blind spot in their life they're not aware of, you gently and lovingly tell them the truth about it. And as soon as you realize that the relationship will not end in marriage, you end it right then, instead of wasting their time or cruelly and falsely building up their hopes.

You leave them better than you found them. Literally, you want their future spouse to be glad that their new husband or wife dated you first. Think about that. That's a revolutionary idea. That's completely countercultural. Instead of evil exes and broken hearts, we'd have old friends who lovingly, intentionally helped us become better people. My friends Marshall and Alison are such a great example of this. When they were dating, Alison told herself that if Marshall did not become her husband, then she still wanted to have helped him become more like Christ. She prayed he would become more ready for his eventual bride than he was before meeting her. She didn't want to be on the list of the baggage he would take with him into another relationship.

The thing is, now they *are* married to each other, so the person she was helping him become better for was herself. Sometimes it turns out that way. It might take a few tries, but at some point you'll find yourself in the one relationship where you don't have to break up.

And then what do you do? Read on. . . .

11

You Know When You Know

THE LIE: getting married is too big a decision to make, and it requires some kind of magical sense that you are destined to be together.

THE TRUTH: you don't have to wait on fate.

When you get engaged, and people first notice that sparkling glint of a precious stone on the girl's left hand, there is always a two-step response. The first step is to tell you both "Congratulations!" often accompanied by inspecting the rock. The second step is to ask, "How did he do it?" or "How did you propose?"

Everyone loves a good engagement story. Correction: every woman seems to love a good engagement story. Women love to hear about the romantic setting, the timing, and the creativity that went into the proposal. Men often like to hear about it to get ideas, but secretly they hope the story is not *too* good so that the bar is not set very high for when they eventually propose.

To appease both camps, I thought I'd share my proposal story. About eighteen years ago, I was dating a young lady named Monica, and it was getting pretty serious. Sometimes it was seriously good, and sometimes seriously bad. But she was also my best friend's sister, and I loved her family. I realized that breaking up wouldn't go too well for me, because I would lose Monica *and* all these other people I cared about. And if we weren't going to break up, maybe I should just marry her. Romantic, right?

If you're going to ask a woman to marry you, and you live in the United States of America in the twenty-first century, that means you need to purchase a ring. Culturally, that's just how we are expected to do things. If you're a man, and you want to get engaged, you buy a rock. I didn't know if I was going to propose next week, next month, or next year, but sooner or later I was going to need to make that purchase, so I went online and started researching my options on eBay (because that's where everyone goes to buy an engagement ring, right? No? Just me?).

There was one ring that, according to the description, was appraised at $23,000. That was massively beyond anything I could afford. However, the next bid amount was $1,600. That was about my budget, so I went ahead and bid the $1,600, even though I knew I would surely be outbid before the auction was over.

I went about my life and put the engagement ring thing on hold, knowing I was in no rush. I didn't even think about it for a few days. Then, about a week later, I got an email saying that I'd won an auction. And I thought, *What auction? What did I win? Oh, crud. It was that engagement ring.* I was now contracted to pay $1,600 to somebody in

New York City who I'd never met, for a ring I'd never seen in person, in what could either be an amazing steal or some kind of scam. But the seller had a good feedback rating; it was a reputable company. When I called the listed phone number and said I'd won the ring auction, the seller said, "No, I can't sell you that. The price is too low." I replied, with some choice language (I wasn't following Christ at the time) that he *had* to sell me the ring for that price; it was a legally binding auction. After some back and forth, he finally relented. I sent him the money, and he sent me the ring.

A few days later it arrived on my doorstep in a little box. The delivery guy just left it there, outside my apartment, where anyone could have picked it up and pocketed it. I opened it up and saw the ring sitting there, all sparkly and pretty, and thought, *There's no way this thing is real. I've been had somehow.* But I took it to a local jeweler to have it tested, and the jeweler said it was a real diamond. However, he couldn't tell me for sure what it was worth without sending it off somewhere for an appraisal.

I told him I didn't have time for that. I put the ring in my pocket and headed out from Dallas to Waco. Monica was graduating from college that weekend, and I thought, *I just got her a graduation present.* I also brought some brand-new golf clubs I'd already bought for her, just in case. I had the graduation gift covered: golf clubs or an engagement ring, depending on how the weekend went.

It turned out to be the golf clubs. As I mentioned, I wasn't following Christ at the time, and my decisions that weekend reflected that. We went out partying, I drank too much, and I almost got into a fight. It wasn't the peaceful, romantic, meaningful scene I had always imagined for a marriage proposal, so I just didn't do it.

That's my proposal story: I didn't propose. And it's only by the grace of God that I didn't. Because if I had pulled that ring out of my pocket that weekend, she would've said yes, and it would have been a nightmare. In fact, there were people in our lives at that time—people who loved us both and wanted what was best for us—saying, "Hey, you guys should break up. Your relationship is a disaster. You two shouldn't be getting married; you shouldn't even be together at all."

But there's a sequel to that story. About a year later, Monica and I went out to dinner with a group of family and friends. The group included some of those same people who had previously said there was no way we should even date, let alone get married. And there, in front of people who cared for us and loved us enough to tell us hard truths, I got down on one knee and pulled out that ring I'd been holding on to for a year. And as Monica said yes, everyone stood up and applauded. The people who had encouraged us to break up now enthusiastically gave their approval to our engagement.

What changed? Why was engagement a terrible idea for us one year and a wise decision the next? And if you are dating and are at the point of considering marriage, how can you tell if it is a good idea for you?

You Know When You Know ... Or?

The common advice for deciding whether you should marry someone is, "You know when you know." But that barely qualifies as advice at all. What it basically says is that you will automatically and magically realize when you are with the person you should marry. In other words, it's not a decision, it's a realization. This implies that if you have any doubts about it, or it is something you have to carefully weigh and decide, then you don't really "know" and therefore shouldn't get married.

That's not how it works at all. Sure, some people can feel like they "just know," but that is only a feeling, and feelings change. Considering the divorce rate, about half of the people who "know" they should get married later "know" they made a mistake.

If you "just know" you should be married to a particular person, my question to you would be, *How* do you know? What information are you basing this knowledge on? What other trusted people in your life are affirming that it is a good idea for you to get married? And if you do get married, are you both committed to staying together and working things out even when (not if) things don't turn out exactly like you had dreamed?

In reality, getting married is a choice. It is a decision you have to make. Just like any other decision, you have to gather information and weigh the pros and cons. It happens to be a really big decision, one that will have massive implications for how the rest of your life will go. But it's not *too* big a decision. You can make a wise choice. You can "know," with some confidence, whether it is a good idea to get married—based on facts, not feelings.

The Foundation to Build On

The biggest fact you need to know is whether you are both fully devoted followers of Christ.

This is what changed for me in the year I held on to that ring. The reason our relationship was transformed was because I was transformed.

After I didn't propose during that graduation weekend, I went back to Dallas and initially continued the same patterns. But then, at the bar one Saturday evening, someone invited me to a church. I stumbled into church the next morning, still a bit hungover, and I heard the gospel of Jesus Christ explained clearly. I heard that my pornography addiction, cocaine use, partying, drinking, clubbing, use of women—Jesus died for all of it. God loved me so much that he sent his Son to die for my sins, and he defeated death. I didn't have to waste my life with those sins or pay for those sins with my life, because Someone else already did. That message captivated my heart, and I submitted my life to Christ. I let him drive. I started listening to what his will was for my life. Through that, he began to deal with all of my bad habits and the destructive patterns I was addicted to. How I treated Monica changed. We stopped sleeping together and started going to church together. Instead of building our relationship on feelings and physical intimacy, tossed up and down by the manic highs and manic lows, we started building our relationship on the solid foundation of Jesus Christ. And with our lives built on that Rock, it finally made sense for me to kneel before Monica and offer her a rock.

The surest and simplest way to ensure a successful marriage is to be confident both of you are fully committed to following Christ first. I'm not saying this means your marriage will then be free from troubles; the Bible actually promises that "those who marry will face many troubles in this life" (1 Cor. 7:28). But, when you are fully following Christ, you won't bring unnecessary troubles (such as addictions, abuse, or adultery) onto yourselves, and you will be able to work together through the troubles that do occur. No marriage has ever ended in divorce when both spouses were fully following God. I can say that with confidence, because divorce itself would be evidence that at least one spouse was not following God's will; it is God's will that people remain married[a] and work through any conflict that arises.

If both of you are fully devoted followers of Christ, desire to get married to each other, and are committed to making marriage work, you should get married. It's a simple decision at that point.

It is easy to know whether those things are true for yourself; the harder part is knowing if they are true for the person you want to marry. Even if they say it is true, can you trust them? There is a lot riding on this decision, and when you agree to marry someone, you give them a massive amount of power over your life. In effect, you're saying, "I'm going to allow you to be either the biggest blessing or the biggest curse on my life. I'm trusting that you'll decide to be a blessing and will put in the relational work required for that to be the case. But I'm also committing to staying by your side even if you decide to be a curse."

How do you know if you can trust them? Sometimes they will outright tell you they are untrustworthy: they will say divorce is an option for them, or they are not willing to obey

a. Matthew 19:4–6: "'Haven't you read,' he replied, 'that at the beginning the Creator "made them male and female," and said, "For this reason a man will leave his father and mother and be united to his wife, and the two will become one flesh"? So they are no longer two, but one flesh. Therefore what God has joined together, let no one separate.'"

God's commands or listen to biblical wisdom. If that's the case, you need to believe them when they say those things (and break up). But assuming they are saying the right things, how can you be sure they are sincere?

With the engagement ring I bought, there were things the jeweler could look at to see if it was genuine. He could test it to see if the diamond was real or if it was an imitation that just looked like the real thing. That's what dating is for: you want to observe their life enough to be confident that they are committed. You date just long enough to figure that out, and then you make the decision to get married.

Get Outside Advice

One way you can gain confidence more quickly is to have trusted advisers who can vouch for your potential spouse's character. Maybe you haven't known your boyfriend or girl-friend for years, but *they* have. They can testify as to whether your significant other is the kind of person he or she claims to be.

In chapter 7, I talked about dating in community and the importance of getting (and listening to) advice from wise counselors. This definitely applies to deciding whether to get married. It's the biggest earthly decision you will ever make, so it is the one you most need to discuss with your community first. If you (or your potential spouse) are living in isolation and don't have a church community to turn to, that is itself a red flag and a sign you should not proceed. "For lack of guidance a nation falls"—or a future marriage fails—"but victory is won through many advisers" (Prov. 11:14).

Besides each of you going to your community, I'm also a huge fan of people going through premarital counseling. It is far better than postmarital counseling—the whole "ounce of prevention is worth a pound of cure" thing—and makes it less likely that you would need couple's counseling after marriage. Some churches offer premarital classes; if your church does not, see if there is a class offered somewhere else in your community.[b]

No Surprises

If you hear me talking about marrying someone who is a fully devoted follower of Christ and think, *There's got to be more to it than that,* this is also where premarital classes can help. Monica and I have provided two-on-two premarital counseling to a number of engaged couples ourselves. A big part of any premarital preparation is discussing important questions, decisions, and expectations with your future spouse. We've found this to be hugely helpful, both in our own marriage and in the marriages of the people we counsel. Although any two Christ followers can commit to each other and make marriage work, the more aligned you are on your expectations and goals, the easier it is. You want to know what you are signing up for and avoid any unnecessary surprises.

An example would be the previously mentioned couple who lived together before the wedding yet never disclosed the amount of debt they were bringing into the marriage.

b. If you can't make it to a class, my friend Scott Kedersha (who, for years, led a premarital ministry called Merge) has written a book called *Ready or Knot?: 12 Conversations Every Couple Needs to Have before Marriage.* It includes most of the material covered in his premarital classes. I would still encourage you to get in-person counseling, but this book is a good additional resource.

That's not a good surprise. Or, early on in our own marriage, Monica and I discovered we had some different expectations when it came to having children. I wanted to wait at least two years before having kids. But for Monica, being a mother was probably her highest priority in life. (And for good reason; having now seen how great she is at being a mother, it is clear to me that God wired her for the role.) As I pushed her to delay starting a family together, I slowly began to realize I was robbing her of something she dearly wanted. We weren't fully aligned on that important issue, and it temporarily caused disappointment and sadness for her.

What do you need to discuss together before marriage? The list is long, but here are the broad categories of what I would consider essential topics.

- **Beliefs.** This is listed first because it is the most important thing. You can have different hobbies or root for different sports teams and still have the makings of a great marriage. But your beliefs are essential to who you are. They are at the core of everything you do in life. Don't get hitched unless you are equally yoked.

- **Finances.** Arguments about how to manage money are consistently cited as a top reason people get divorced.[1] So, at some point in your dating relationship, you need to talk at length about how you're going to handle earnings, savings, spending, and debt. Remember: after marriage, it is not *your* money or *their* debt; it is *our* money and *our* debt. The two of you become one unit financially. As part of your marriage preparation, you should put together a combined monthly budget and balance sheet.

- **Family.** When you get married, your spouse's family also becomes *your* family, and your family becomes theirs. You need to discuss ahead of time the roles your in-laws will play in your lives, figure out how and where you will spend the holidays, and have an idea of what your family traditions will look like after combining families.

- **Children.** Do you both want to have children? If so, when and how many? How do you feel about adoption or fostering? If you have kids, how will you raise them? Will one of you be a stay-at-home parent? I'm now fully in favor of kids—they are a gift from God[c]—but you need to make sure you are on the same page together. If you want kids, you don't want to commit to spending your whole life with someone who doesn't want them, or vice versa.

- **Goals.** What do you want to accomplish together? What kind of life do you want to live? Where do you want to live? If one of you wants to live in an uptown high-rise and the other feels called to be a missionary in a rural part of Uganda, you might not be the best match for each other. You can still compromise, but you need to agree ahead of time what your plans will be together.

- **Expectations.** If you expect marriage to look a certain way, and your future spouse expects something different, one (or both) of you is going to end up disappointed. So, it's important to talk through all your expectations and come to an agreement on how

c. Psalm 127:3: "Children are a heritage from the LORD, offspring a reward from him."

things are going to work. This includes everything from how you divvy up cooking and cleaning to how you spend your vacation time.

- **Sex.** This might seem awkward to talk about, but it is also very important to discuss key questions, such as: How often do you expect to have sex? What things will be considered inbounds or out of bounds for you sexually? Because it is an intimate subject, I would recommend starting with general discussions on this topic and waiting until after engagement (when you are sure you are going to get married) to get into specific details.

- **Conflict.** How will you work through conflict together? Are you someone who tries to withdraw and avoid conflict, or do you confront it aggressively and escalate arguments? Knowing that, how will you work to overcome those patterns and peacefully resolve conflict together?

- **What ifs.** There are many things that can happen in life after marriage; some are more likely than others. I think it is a good idea to discuss together how you will respond in different hypothetical scenarios. I call them "what ifs." What if you lose your job? What if one of you is diagnosed with cancer? What if you are infertile? What if your spouse has an affair? What if you become famous? There are hundreds of possibilities. Figure out how you would respond (and keep your marriage healthy) ahead of time, and you will be prepared when or if any of those things happen.

- **Divorce.** Related to the "what ifs," you should talk about whether divorce is an option in any scenario. I believe the answer should be no. For starters, research shows that divorce does not make people happier. If you are unhappy being married, you will, on average, be just as unhappy being single or marrying someone else.[2] More importantly, though, it is always God's desire that we would seek forgiveness and be reconciled. And in the standard marriage vows there is no allowance for divorce; you are vowing to stay together "for better or worse," "in sickness and in health," and so on, "until death do us part." I always say that if divorce is an option, then you really need to write that into your vows: "For better or worse, unless you cheat on me with my best friend," or whatever the exception might be. I'm not kidding. Don't make a vow unless you mean it. If you don't want to include divorce in your vows, then make sure you are both committed to making marriage work no matter what.

Prepare for Marriage, Not a Wedding

All of this is designed to help you prepare for marriage. One thing a lot of engaged couples get wrong is that they focus on preparing for a wedding and neglect to prepare for marriage.

I know that many of you, especially many women, have been dreaming about your wedding day since your preschool days. I know you have a Pinterest board filled with dresses and floral arrangements and cakes that cost more than your car. However, it is just one day. You will have, hopefully, *twenty thousand* days of marriage after that. Don't spend the majority of your time preparing for just .005 percent of your marriage.

I would also recommend you don't spend the majority of your money on a wedding. I know weddings can be expensive no matter what you do; I'm just saying you shouldn't be so focused on having an impressive party that you mortgage your future to pay for it. One study found that the people who spent the most on their wedding were also the most likely to divorce.[3] The reason could be because of the financial stress it puts on the marriage, if the couple is paying for the wedding themselves, but it could also be a symptom of wanting a wedding more than wanting a marriage.

The same study showed that having more people attend a wedding generally lowered the chance of divorce. It probably shouldn't be a surprise that weddings with no guests (only the couple) have a high divorce rate; apparently what happens in Vegas doesn't last. But having more people at your wedding shows that you have a community and family around you who support your decision to get married. It also shows that "big" doesn't have to equate to "expensive"; the goal should be celebrating with those you care about rather than impressing your guests.

The same logic applies for engagement rings. Guys, don't try to win her heart with the size of the diamond. That should not be the reason she marries you. There is nothing wrong with getting her something she will like, but be responsible. Don't go into debt. Remember that you can always upgrade the stone later for an anniversary, if you want. (Or you can give eBay a try.)

I've met many people who have delayed getting married for months or years solely to afford a better ring or a more extravagant wedding. Man, that's a bad tradeoff. They're literally valuing the ring or the wedding more than the marriage, saying it is worth more to them than spending all that time as man and wife. Don't make that trade. If the two of you are ready to get married, then get married already.

How Long?

I often get questions about how long a couple should date each other before getting married. The answer: long enough to know that you would make good spouses for each other, and no longer. There is no set time period, because it depends on the situation.

You should be wary of getting married *too* quickly, because it is likely a sign you are focused on feelings. You don't spend the time to get all the facts because you are "in love," they are "the one," or you "just know." That being said, if you have known the person for a long time before dating, or you can "check their references" through trusted advisers who already know them well, then a short timeline could make sense. If you have biblical community around you, and they all agree your marriage is a good idea, then there is no reason to drag it out.

It is just as concerning when a couple takes too long to get married. I'm talking about people who are adults and who could marry at any time, but instead stay in a dating relationship for years without deciding to tie the knot. That is problematic because it raises questions of *why* you haven't gotten married. Is it because you realize there are serious issues in the relationship, and you know you probably shouldn't marry this person, but you are afraid of breaking up and winding up alone? Is it because you have made the mistake of already living together, and so you (or the person you are with) see no reason to get married? Studies back up the idea that getting married too quickly or too slowly are both potentially problematic.[4]

And once you do propose, how long should your engagement be? Long enough to plan a wedding and allow your guests to make plans to attend, but no longer. When you get engaged, you're presumably already ready to get married; you're not still figuring that part out. You've verbally agreed to marry each other. You could technically get married that day, if you wanted. Doing so wouldn't be impulsive, because you've already made the real decision over a longer period of time. Of course, your family and friends need a "heads up" in order to attend the wedding and make any necessary travel plans, and the wedding itself, no matter how simple, does take some time to plan. I'm not suggesting you should get married immediately. But if it takes you more than half a year to plan a wedding, I'm worried you might be putting more thought into the wedding than into the marriage. You're also missing out on months you could have spent married—time together as husband and wife that you'll never get back.

Build a Life Together

In past generations—almost every past generation, back to the beginning of time—marriage was the foundation of adult life.

I'm not saying you had to get married in order to be an adult, because not all adults got married. It's never been a requirement. But those who did get married didn't wait as long. They got married younger—about 25 percent younger, if you compare our grandparents' generation to today.[d]

They were able to marry younger because they had a different view of adulthood and marriage. People would see that being an adult took work. They were just starting their career. They didn't have much money or many possessions, and they probably had debt. They also had desires, and they didn't want to be alone. They recognized that "adulting" was hard and would be easier if they had help. So they looked around—literally looked around, without the help of dating apps or massive social networks—and found a like-minded person of the opposite sex within their relatively small circle of acquaintances. And after vetting each other with the help of family and friends, they would get married. They would come together, help each other navigate adulthood, and build a life together. Marriage was the foundation.

Today there seems to be this pressure to have everything together first. You need to already have the house, be advanced in your career, make this much money, have paid off your debt, and be able to afford a multicarat ring before you get married. Instead of being the foundation of adult life, marriage is like the furnishings. It's like a new sofa or a big-screen TV. It's an accessory you can now add to your established life. And, as either a cause or an effect of that trend, people who do get married are doing so later in life.

There are some good reasons to wait before getting married. Don't rush into marriage, and don't even date until marriage is a possibility for you. Make sure your whole life is first and foremost built on the foundation of faith in Christ.

---

d. As mentioned in the introduction, the average age of marriage today is 28.9 years, compared to 21.5 years in 1960.

And if you have issues you need to resolve, so that you are not bringing baggage into marriage, work on those first (and start working on them now).

But don't delay marriage for the wrong reasons. Don't think you have to already have the picket fence in the suburbs. Don't buy the lie that your wedding has to look like a Disney fairy tale. Don't make marriage optional because you're already living with someone in a pretend marriage. Don't live in a fantasy world; make it a reality.

The Next Steps

If you want to get married, then I want to see you get married and be married well. Whatever the next step is toward that goal, make the decision to do it now.

And what is your next step? Just to recap, here's a super-simple version of the steps to take.

If you are a man:

1. Have a thriving relationship with Jesus.
2. Overcome any harmful addictions, troublesome baggage, or any other glaring problems that would make you unfit to be a good husband.
3. Identify the godliest single woman you know. Walk up to her and ask her out on a date.
4. If she says no, check yourself and realize that you're still alive. You're going to be OK. Repeat step three with the *next* godliest woman you know.
5. If she says yes, and the date goes well (meaning that there are no red flags and she still seems like someone

you'd like to get to know better), ask her on another date. If, on the other hand, the date makes you realize you are no longer interested in her, then gently break up and go back to step three.

6. Repeat step five as many times as needed until you (and the people you trust as advisers) feel confident you should ask her to marry you. And then ask her to marry you.

If you are a woman:

1. Have a thriving relationship with Jesus.
2. Overcome any harmful addictions, troublesome baggage, or any other glaring problems that would make you unfit to be a good wife.
3. This is optional, but if you are interested in a godly man, feel free to let him know you are interested.
4. If a godly single man asks you out on a date (and you've already covered steps one and two), say yes to the date. If someone asks you out who would clearly not be a godly husband, say no.
5. If the date goes well (meaning there are no red flags and he still seems like someone you'd like to get to know better), and he asks you out again, say yes again. If, on the other hand, the date makes you realize you are no longer interested in him, then gently break up and go back to step three or four.
6. Repeat step five as many times as needed until you (and the people you trust as advisers) feel confident

he is a man you would want to marry. If so, and he proposes, you again say yes.

Not everyone will complete all these steps, and that's fine; go back and read chapter 2 again. But most people will get married at some point, so read on to learn what happens next.

12

Happily Ever After

THE LIE: marriage is a fairy tale.

THE TRUTH: marriage doesn't save you from troubles—
but it can provide a preview of what the real "happily
ever after" will be like.

Imagine that you meet someone and decide to marry them. You have your dream wedding and then head off to an island honeymoon. Everything is perfect. But then, while still on your honeymoon, your new spouse becomes ill and is diagnosed with a debilitating lifelong disease. Suddenly, your lot in life is to take care of all their needs: feeding them, bathing them, and changing their diaper. That's your new role. Though you hadn't realized it, when you said "I do," that is what you were saying you would do.

That story is both completely hypothetical and completely real. It is hypothetical because it is highly unlikely to happen. But it is real because it *does* happen on rare occasions. With billions of marriages throughout history and many millions of new weddings each year,[1] rare things do end up becoming reality. In fact, although I don't know anyone personally with that exact circumstance, I did see news stories about a local bride who was paralyzed by a rogue wave while at the beach on the fourth day of her Hawaii honeymoon.[2] And we don't have to limit it to just the honeymoon; if you and your spouse both make it to old age together, the odds that one of you will have to care for the other in that way become fairly high. So, although on the one hand, I would never wish that on anyone, on the other hand, I can only hope you are married long enough to have to care for someone in that way—or have them do so for you.[a]

If you are not ready and willing to care for your future spouse "in sickness and in health," or when "for better" becomes "for worse," then you probably have a fairy-tale misconception of what marriage is really like. You are also likely seeking marriage for purely selfish reasons—wanting to be loved by someone but not to truly love them in return.

The Truth about Marriage

"Happily ever after." I think that is what we are all seeking, not just in love but also in life. That's the main myth. We all just want to be happy. And we are told over and over, from our earliest childhood, that living "happily ever after" begins with marriage. The "after" part refers to right after the wedding, as the new bride and groom ride off in their carriage while being literally cheered on by a crowd of adoring wedding guests.

a. Not to mention that if you have kids, you will absolutely have to feed them, bathe them, and change their diapers for at least a couple of years. That is another part of marriage you are most likely signing up for.

But that cheering stops as soon as you leave the parking lot. Real marriage starts right where the fairy tale leaves off. I am not at all saying that marriage is a bad thing or that it is to be avoided. I am a fan of marriage. It's just that if you want your marriage to be successful, you need to have a correct understanding of what it is you are signing up for. Even the best of marriages has troubles. God's Word guarantees it; 1 Corinthians 7:28 says that "those who marry will face many troubles in this life." In fact, the person who wrote that verse—the apostle Paul, who was a bachelor himself—was kind of trying to convince the Corinthians not to get married, for that very reason. Of course, single people also have troubles in this life, as Paul would have been well aware of himself—he experienced beatings, stoning, imprisonment, hunger, shipwrecks (2 Cor. 11:23–27), snakebite (Acts 28:3), sickness (Gal. 4:13–14), and eventual martyrdom. He's not saying single life is carefree. It is just that everyone has troubles in life, and in marriage you share the troubles of two people.

The goal of life is not to avoid troubles but to glorify God in the way we handle them (1 Cor. 10:31).

What Are You Signing Up For?

When you get married, you make a promise. The promise is not that you will always be happy, or even that you will always be able to make your spouse happy. You can't guarantee that, because you don't have full control over it; you'd end up breaking that promise. Instead, the things you are promising are things you do have full control over: serving sacrificially, striving for oneness, and sticking with it.

- **Serving sacrificially.** In marriage, you commit to loving each other selflessly. It is an act of service, not a feeling. Spouses are called to submit to each other, be considerate of each other, and treat each other with respect (Eph. 5:21–33; 1 Pet. 3:1–7). You should care for your spouse the way you care for yourself and your own body (Eph. 5:28–29).
- **Striving for oneness.** Speaking of bodies, in marriage your body is no longer fully your own; it is something you mutually share with your spouse (1 Cor. 7:2–5). You are now one flesh (Gen. 2:24), and are to work together as one unit. As my wife and I regularly have to remind each other, we are on the same team, working together for common goals. We must constantly work to develop intimacy and oneness in our relationship.
- **Sticking with it.** This is what you make a solemn vow to do when you get married: to stay together *no matter what*, in any circumstance, "until death do us part." That is why we have to serve sacrificially and strive for oneness.

That is what you are signing up for when you get married. It's pretty simple, really. People say that marriage is hard work—and it absolutely is—but it is mostly hard as a result of one (or both) spouses failing to do those three things. When you are both working together and doing your part, marriage really is a beautiful thing.

In fact, marriage is meant to be a picture of the most beautiful thing to ever happen.

Holy Ever After

In the hypothetical-but-also-real example given at the start of this chapter, no one would really want to have to care for an invalid spouse. That is truly sacrificial work: doing for someone else what they can't do themselves, with no possibility of them ever returning the favor or doing anything to really earn your attention and care. That's true love. However, although you might not want to do that for someone, I guarantee you want someone who would be willing to do that for you. Because there are two sides to this story: the one person who makes the necessary sacrifices and the other person who absolutely needs that help in order to live. In marriage, two people agree to take on either role when or if it ever happens to them.

You may never need someone to care for you in that way in this life. I mean, you could die in a car crash tomorrow and go instantly from "healthy" to "dead." It's possible, and in that case, you wouldn't need anyone to care for you. But you would need something else, because death is not the end.

Marriage is a picture of God's love for us, because there is nothing we could ever do to earn his love. None of us are perfect; everyone has sinned at some point, and most of us probably do so several times each day. Even if you were close to perfect, there is nothing you can do that would really benefit God or cause him to owe you a favor. He created everything—including your life, your abilities, and your time—so anything you could possibly give him would just be returning stuff that was already his. That's one of the problems with most every religion: they are all about earning favor with a god who gets no benefit from anything you do.

However, God chooses to love us—perfectly and forever. In much the same way a married person commits to sacrificially serving their spouse and pursuing oneness with them no matter what they may do (or fail to do) in return, God sticks with us despite our mistakes.

A perfect, holy God can't just ignore sin and condone the pain it causes. Sin requires payment; something must be done to atone for wrongdoing. Since we couldn't make up for it and earn his good graces in our own lives, God used his life. He sent his Son, Jesus, to suffer the punishment for our sins on the cross. We could never earn such a sacrifice; he offered it lovingly as a free gift. And if you accept that gift—if you admit you have sinned and therefore need God's forgiveness—you can live forever together with him.

That's why heaven is described as a wedding feast, and the church is known as the bride of Christ.[b] Marriage helps us understand heaven, even though being married to an imperfect human may sometimes feel far from being heaven on earth.

The Fairy-Tale Ending

In a way, you can get the fairy-tale ending. You can live happily ever after, forever after. And you don't necessarily have to get married on this earth to do it.

Marriage is an important thing in this life, but it is far from being the ultimate thing. Make sure you know the One you'll be "married" to forever. Find someone else who is already "married" well to Jesus, and then spend this life pursuing him together.

b. Revelation 19:6–9 and 21:1–5; also Mark 2:19–20; 2 Corinthians 11:2; and Ephesians 5:25–32.

Notes

Introduction

1. "Millennials in Adulthood," Pew Research Center, March 7, 2014, http://www.pewsocialtrends.org/2014/03/07/millennials-in-adulthood/.
2. "Shifting Life Milestones across Ages: A Matter of Preference or Circumstance?" Stanford Center on Longevity, February 6, 2018, http://longevity.stanford.edu/2018/02/06/milestones/.
3. "Historical Marital Status Tables," United States Census Bureau, November 2019, https://www.census.gov/data/tables/time-series/demo/families/marital.html.
4. Paul R. Amato, "Research on Divorce: Continuing Trends and New Developments," *Journal of Marriage and Family*, June 18, 2010, https://onlinelibrary.wiley.com/doi/abs/10.1111/j.1741-3737.2010.00723.x. Also Bella DePaulo, "What Is the Divorce Rate, Really?" *Psychology Today*, February 2, 2017, https://www.psychologytoday.com/us/blog/living-single/201702/what-is-the-divorce-rate-really.
5. Larry Getlen, "The Fascinating History of How Courtship Became 'Dating.'" *New York Post*, May 15, 2016, https://nypost.com/2016/05/15/the-fascinating-history-of-how-courtship-became-dating/.

Chapter 2 Singleness Is a Problem to Be Fixed

1. Gary Chapman, *The Five Love Languages: How to Express Heartfelt Commitment to Your Mate* (Chicago: Northfield Publishing, 1992).
2. Charles Pope, "Marriage and Family at the Time of Jesus," *Community in Mission*, March 26, 2017, http://blog.adw.org/2017/03/marriage-family-time-jesus/.

3. Chris Lowney, "Hey, Pope Francis, Where Are All the Married Saints?" CNN, February 12, 2015, https://www.cnn.com/2015/02/12/living/valentines-day-saints/index.html.

Chapter 3 The One

1. The story is in Plato, *The Symposium*, written in 360 BC. See "Symposium by Plato," *The Internet Classics Archive*, accessed June 30, 2020, http://classics.mit.edu/Plato/symposium.html.

2. Randall Munroe, "Soul Mates," *What If?*, August 28, 2012, https://what-if.xkcd.com/9/.

3. Richard Alleyne, "Romantic Comedies Make Us 'Unrealistic about Relationships', Claim Scientists," *The Telegraph*, December 15, 2008, https://www.telegraph.co.uk/culture/film/3776923/Romantic-comedies-make-us-unrealistic-about-relationships-claim-scientists.html. Also Eben Harrell, "Are Romantic Movies Bad For You?" *Time*, December 23, 2008, http://content.time.com/time/health/article/0,8599,1868389,00.html.

4. Mark Banschick, "The High Failure Rate of Second and Third Marriages," *Psychology Today*, February 6, 2012, https://www.psychologytoday.com/us/blog/the-intelligent-divorce/201202/the-high-failure-rate-second-and-third-marriages.

Chapter 4 Love at First Sight

1. Sharom Romm, "Beauty through History," *Washington Post*, January 27, 1987, https://www.washingtonpost.com/archive/lifestyle/wellness/1987/01/27/beauty-through-history/301f7256-0f6b-403e-abec-f36c0a3ec313.

2. Romm, "Beauty through History."

3. Jacqueline Howard, "The History of the 'Ideal' Woman and Where That Has Left Us," CNN, March 9, 2018, https://www.cnn.com/2018/03/07/health/body-image-history-of-beauty-explainer-intl/index.html.

4. Howard, "The History of the 'Ideal' Woman."

5. Howard, "The History of the 'Ideal' Woman."

6. Dina Spector, "8 Scientifically Proven Reasons Life Is Better If You're Beautiful," *Business Insider*, June 12, 2013, https://www.businessinsider.com/studies-show-the-advantages-of-being-beautiful-2013-6.

7. Derek Thompson, "The Financial Benefits of Being Beautiful," *The Atlantic*, January 11, 2014, https://www.theatlantic.com/business/archive/2014/01/the-financial-benefits-of-being-beautiful/282975/.

8. Sophia Mitrokostas, "10 Benefits of Being Attractive, According to Science," *Business Insider*, December 7, 2018, https://www.insider.com/benefits-of-being-attractive-science-2018-12.

9. Susan Trompeter, Ricki Bettencourt, and Elizabeth Barrett-Connor, "Sexual Activity and Satisfaction in Healthy Community-Dwelling Older Women," *American Journal of Medicine*, January 2012, https://www.amj med.com/article/S0002-9343(11)00655-3/fulltext. Also Emily DiNuzzo, "This Is the Surprising Age When You'll Have the Best Sex of Your Life," *The Healthy*, April 26, 2019, https://www.thehealthy.com/sex/surprising -age-best-sex-life-survey/.

10. Vinita Mehta, "Do Beautiful People Have Better Relationships?" *Psychology Today*, April 23, 2017, https://www.psychologytoday.com/ca /blog/head-games/201704/do-beautiful-people-have-better-relationships.

11. Dan Kopf, "These Statistics Show Why It's So Hard to Be an Average Man on Dating Apps," *Quartz*, August 15, 2017, https://qz.com /1051462/these-statistics-show-why-its-so-hard-to-be-an-average-man -on-dating-apps/. Also "Tinder Experiments II: Guys, Unless You Are Really Hot You Are Probably Better Off Not Wasting Your Time on Tinder—A Quantitative Socio-Economic Study," *Medium*, March 24, 2015, https://medium.com/@worstonlinedater/tinder-experiments-ii -guys-unless-you-are-really-hot-you-are-probably-better-off-not-wasting -your-2ddf370a6e9a.

Chapter 5 Love Is a Feeling

1. Walter Isaacson and Woody Allen, "The Heart Wants What It Wants," *Time*, August 31, 1992, http://content.time.com/time/magazine /article/0,9171,976345,00.html.

2. The saying "Change your playmates and your playground" is common throughout many kinds of recovery programs. A version of the quote appears in the *Narcotics Anonymous Basic Text*, which may be where it originated.

Chapter 6 A Perfect Match

1. Michael J. Rosenfeld, Reuben J. Thomas, and Sonia Hausen, "Disintermediating Your Friends: How Online Dating in the United States Displaces Other Ways of Meeting," *Proceedings of the National Academy of Sciences*, September 3, 2019, https://www.pnas.org/content/early /2019/08/19/1908630116.

2. Rosenfeld, Thomas, and Hausen, "Disintermediating Your Friends."

Chapter 7 Playing Games

1. University of Montreal, "Women Outperform Men When Identifying Emotions," *ScienceDaily*, October 21, 2009, https://www.sciencedaily

.com/releases/2009/10/091021125133.htm. Also B. Schiffer et al., "Why Don't Men Understand Women? Altered Neural Networks for Reading the Language of Male and Female Eyes," *PLoS ONE*, April 10, 2013, https://doi.org/10.1371/journal.pone.0060278.

Chapter 8 No Strings Attached

1. Randy Olson, "144 Years of Marriage and Divorce in 1 Chart," *Randal S. Olson*, June 15, 2015, http://www.randalolson.com/2015/06/15/144-years-of-marriage-and-divorce-in-1-chart/.

2. Joseph Chamie, "Out-of-Wedlock Births Rise Worldwide," *Yale University*, March 16, 2017, https://yaleglobal.yale.edu/content/out-wedlock-births-rise-worldwide.

3. David Sivak, "Fact Check: Have There Been 60 Million Abortions Since Roe v. Wade?" Checkyourfact.com, July 3, 2018, https://checkyourfact.com/2018/07/03/fact-check-60-million-abortions/.

4. "New CDC Report: STDs Continue to Rise in the U.S." Centers for Disease Control and Prevention, October 8, 2019, https://www.cdc.gov/nchhstp/newsroom/2019/2018-STD-surveillance-report-press-release.html.

5. "Incidence, Prevalence, and Cost of Sexually Transmitted Infections in the United States," Centers for Disease Control and Prevention, February 2013, https://www.cdc.gov/std/stats/sti-estimates-fact-sheet-feb-2013.pdf.

6. Serina Sandhu, "One in Three Women Watch Porn at Least Once a Week, Survey Finds," *The Independent*, October 21, 2015, https://www.independent.co.uk/life-style/love-sex/one-in-three-women-watch-porn-at-least-once-a-week-survey-finds-a6702476.html.

7. "Statistics about Sexual Violence," National Sexual Violence Resource Center, accessed October 27, 2019, https://www.nsvrc.org/sites/default/files/publications_nsvrc_factsheet_media-packet_statistics-about-sexual-violence_0.pdf.

8. Rhitu Chatterjee, "A New Survey Finds 81 Percent of Women Have Experienced Sexual Harassment," NPR, February 21, 2018, https://www.npr.org/sections/thetwo-way/2018/02/21/587671849/a-new-survey-finds-eighty-percent-of-women-have-experienced-sexual-harassment.

9. Stephanie Pappas, "Oxytocin: Facts about the 'Cuddle Hormone.'" *Live Science*, June 4, 2015, https://www.livescience.com/42198-what-is-oxytocin.html.

10. Lee Ann Obringer, "How Love Works," *How Stuff Works*, February 12, 2005, https://people.howstuffworks.com/love.htm.

11. Mary Parke, "Are Married Parents Really Better for Children? What Research Says about the Effects of Family Structure on Child

Well-Being," Center for Law and Social Policy, May 2003, https://www.clasp
.org/sites/default/files/public/resources-and-publications/states/0086.pdf.
Also Jane Anderson, "The Impact of Family Structure on the Health of
Children: Effects of Divorce," *The Linacre Quarterly*, November 2014,
https://www.ncbi.nlm.nih.gov/pmc/articles/PMC4240051/.

12. "How Effective Is Contraception at Preventing Pregnancy?" *NHS*, June
30, 2017, https://www.nhs.uk/conditions/contraception/how-effective
-contraception/.

13. Bill Hendrick, "Benefits in Delaying Sex until Marriage," WebMD,
December 28, 2019, https://www.webmd.com/sex-relationships/news
/20101227/theres-benefits-in-delaying-sex-until-marriage#1.

14. Stephanie Pappas, "The History of Pornography No More Prudish
Than the Present," *Live Science*, October 11, 2010, https://www.livescience
.com/8748-history-pornography-prudish-present.html.

15. Guy Kelly, "The Scary Effects of Pornography: How the 21st Century's Acute Addiction Is Rewiring Our Brains," *Telegraph*, September
11, 2017, https://www.telegraph.co.uk/men/thinking-man/scary-effects
-pornography-21st-centurys-accute-addiction-rewiring/.

16. Grant Hilary Brenner, "4 Ways Porn Use Causes Problems," *Psychology Today*, March 5, 2018, https://www.psychologytoday.com/us/blog
/experimentations/201803/4-ways-porn-use-causes-problems.

17. Jason S. Carroll, "The Porn Gap: Gender Differences in Pornography Use in Couple Relationships," *Institute for Family Studies*, October
4, 2017, https://ifstudies.org/blog/the-porn-gap-gender-differences-in
-pornography-use-in-couple-relationships.

18. Scott Kedersha, "The Most Important 0.625% of Your Marriage,"
Scott Kedersha, February 16, 2015, https://www.scottkedersha.com/the
-most-important-0-625-of-your-marriage/.

Chapter 9 Try It before You Buy It

1. Benjamin Gurrentz, "Living with an Unmarried Partner Now Common for Young Adults," United States Census Bureau, November 15,
2018, https://www.census.gov/library/stories/2018/11/cohabitaiton-is-up
-marriage-is-down-for-young-adults.html.

2. Scott Stanley and Galena Rhoades, "Premarital Cohabitation Is Still
Associated with Greater Odds of Divorce," *Institute for Family Studies*,
October 17, 2018, https://ifstudies.org/blog/premarital-cohabitation-is
-still-associated-with-greater-odds-of-divorce.

3. Danielle Braff, "Until Honeymoon We Do Part," *New York Times*,
March 13, 2019, https://www.nytimes.com/2019/03/13/fashion/weddings
/until-honeymoon-we-do-part.html.

4. Stanley and Rhoades, "Premarital Cohabitation."

5. Patricia Lee June, "Cohabitation: Effects of Cohabitation on the Men and Women Involved—Part 1 of 2," *American College of Pediatricians*, March 2015, https://acpeds.org/position-statements/cohabitation-part-1-of-2-effects-of-cohabitation-on-the-men-and-women-involved.

6. June, "Cohabitation."

7. Gurrentz, "Living with an Unmarried Partner."

8. Gurrentz, "Living with an Unmarried Partner."

9. Amie Gordon, "The 'Cohabitation Effect': The Consequences of Premarital Cohabitation," *Berkeley Science Review*, August 12, 2012, https://berkeleysciencereview.com/2012/08/the-cohabitation-effect-the-consequences-of-premarital-cohabitation/.

10. Sheri Stritof, "Essential Cohabitation Facts and Statistics," *The Spruce*, August 14, 2019, https://www.thespruce.com/cohabitation-facts-and-statistics-2302236.

11. Rachel Rettner, "More Couples Living Together Outside of Marriage," *Live Science*, April 4, 2013, https://www.livescience.com/28420-cohabiting-marriage-cdc-report.html.

12. Scott Stanley et al., "Sliding versus Deciding: Inertia and the Premarital Cohabitation Effect," *Family Relations*, October 2006, https://onlinelibrary.wiley.com/doi/full/10.1111/j.1741-3729.2006.00418.x.

13. "What Were Common Marriage Customs in Bible Times?" Got Questions.org, July 26, 2019, https://www.gotquestions.org/marriage-customs.html.

14. Joe Pinsker, "The New Long-Distance Relationship," *The Atlantic*, May 14, 2019, https://www.theatlantic.com/family/archive/2019/05/long-distance-relationships/589144/.

Chapter 11 You Know When You Know

1. Jeffrey Dew, Sonya Britt, and Sandra Huston, "Examining the Relationship between Financial Issues and Divorce," *Family Relations*, September 4, 2012, https://onlinelibrary.wiley.com/doi/abs/10.1111/.1741-3729.2012.00715.x.

2. Similarly, research shows that people who divorce and stay single, or divorce and then remarry, end up no happier than unhappy couples who stay married. See "Does Divorce Make People Happy? Findings from a Study of Unhappy Marriages," *Institute of American Values*, accessed June 7, 2019, http://americanvalues.org/search/item.php?id=13.

3. Andrew Francis-Tan and Hugo M. Mialon, "'A Diamond Is Forever' and Other Fairy Tales: The Relationship between Wedding Expenses and

Marriage Duration," *Economic Inquiry*, September 15, 2014, https://papers.ssrn.com/sol3/papers.cfm?abstract_id=2501480.

4. Sylvia Niehuis, Linda Skogrand, and Ted L. Huston, "When Marriages Die: Premarital and Early Marriage Precursors to Divorce," *The Forum for Family and Consumer Issues*, June 2006, https://www.theforum journal.org/2006/06/03/when-marriages-die-premarital-and-early-marr iage-precursors-to-divorce/.

Chapter 12 Happily Ever After

1. In the United States alone, there are over 2,000,000 new marriages each year. See Erin Duffin, "Number of Marriages in the U.S. 1990–2017," *Statista*, April 29, 2019, https://www.statista.com/statistics/195931/number-of-marriages-in-the-united-states-since-1990/.

2. Teresa Woodard, "North Texas Woman Paralyzed Days after Hawaii Wedding Makes Big Strides at Rehab," *WFAA*, October 12, 2018, https://www.wfaa.com/article/news/north-texas-woman-paralyzed-days-after-hawaii-wedding-makes-big-strides-at-rehab/287-603915634.

About the Author

Jonathan "JP" Pokluda is the lead pastor of a church in Waco, Texas, called Harris Creek. For over a decade he led the largest Christian singles gathering in America, The Porch. He's had a front-row seat for watching thousands of relationships form and flourish while others fizzled out. JP's most recent book, *Outdated*, was written after years of observing the changing landscape of dating. He didn't come to understand the grace of the gospel until his early twenties, after being involved in different denominational churches his entire life. This ignited a desire in him to inspire young adults to radically follow Jesus Christ and unleash them to change the world. His bestselling book *Welcome to Adulting* offers Millennials a road map to navigating faith, finding a spouse, finances, and the future. JP's partner in ministry is Monica, his wife of sixteen years, and together they disciple their children Presley, Finley, and Weston.

Kevin McConaghy works as a writer for Watermark Community Church in Dallas, Texas. He has collaborated with JP on writing projects for a number of years, including JP's first book, *Welcome to Adulting*. He and his wife, Juliana, have three children.

JONATHAN POKLUDA

CONNECT WITH JP

 Jonathan Pokluda | @JPokluda | @JPokluda

---

Hopeful romantic,

I know the world is fast-changing and the dating scene can be frustrating. I pray that this resource fills your heart with hope and contentment and offers you clear direction for finding love in the twenty-first century. I write books because I believe God desires to use your generation to heal our land and glorify his name. I don't invest a lot of money in marketing. I simply try and write truths that are helpful. With that said, YOU are my very best advertising. Would you take a picture of yourself with the book and share it? If you tag @jpokluda, I will share your post. Thank you for your prayers and support. I know God has a plan for you, I know his plan is good, and I know his Word is never outdated. I pray you read it in and live it out.

Much love!

JP

YOU'RE AN ADULT . . .
NOW WHAT?

Adulting is hard. But sometimes we make it harder than it has to be. If you're struggling to find a footing in the world of adult life, these witty, non-patronizing guides are for you.

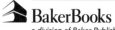

THE BOOK THAT
EVERY PASTOR NEEDS

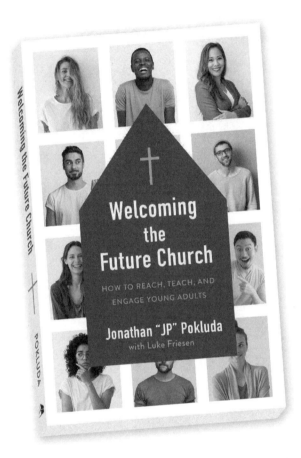

Tomorrow's church is out there, waiting for you to care,
to reach out, to understand their struggles, and to show
them why today's church needs, wants, and cherishes them.
If you want your church to have a future, you have
to be actively reaching the future church.

 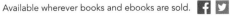

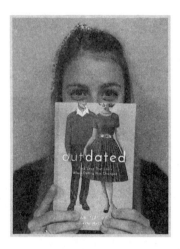

- Become an **#Outdated** ambassador by taking a photo of yourself with the book, like above, and sharing it on your social media platforms.

- Write a book review on your blog or on a retailer site.

- Pick up a copy for friends, family, or anyone who you think would enjoy and be challenged by its message!

- Share this message on Twitter, Facebook, or Instagram:
I loved #OutdatedBook by @JPokluda // @ReadBakerBooks

- Recommend this book for your church, workplace, book club, or class.

- Follow Baker Books on social media and tell us what you like.

 **ReadBakerBooks**

 **ReadBakerBooks**

ReadBakerBooks